MLM
HEART ATTACK
Restart the Heart
and Your Dreams!

Jordan Adler • Orjan Saele
Donna Johnson • Ken Dunn

Foreword by Art Jonak

MLM Heart Attack
Restart the Heart and Your Dreams!

Copyright © 2013 by Jordan Adler, Örjan Saele,
Donna Johnson, and Ken Dunn
All rights reserved.

ISBN: 978-1939268-402

Published by Next Century Publishing
www.NextCenturyPublishing.com

DEDICATION

This book is, without question, undeniably, and purposefully,
for you and your success ...
and we all wish you the absolute best
from the bottom of our hearts.

FOREWORD

"Nobody can go back and start a new beginning... but anyone can start today and make a new ending." — Maria Robinson

It was early 1992. I'd just finished reel-to-reel backups and was heading into the dreaded 4 a.m. hour, halfway through the graveyard shift, when time starts to crawl. The University of Virginia computer department was one, big, freezing, white room. Did the minute hand of the clock just move? Not sure. Hope it did. Four more hours to go. Torture.

I stared into the boxy, monochrome computer monitor, super high-tech at the time. Who was in there? I could connect with the few others around the world with access to this thing called 'email,' but they were mostly people associated with universities... and most of those were asleep.

There was no Facebook or Twitter. Actually, there were no websites, no world wide web, and you could not "www dot anything." Imagine that. But we did have something called 'bulletin boards.' There were a couple dozen topics you could post under where, hopefully, someone else saw your post and replied, creating a connection.

I'd been active in one bulletin board called "alt.business" and since I had just started a network marketing business a little over a year ago, I was looking to connect with other "sharp, business-minded people who kept their options open." Yes, verbiage straight from a *Getting Started Right* manual. And connect I did. It was pretty cool.

One 4 a.m. morning, I decided to start a board just for network marketers like myself. After weeks of requests and formalities, 'alt.business.multi-level' was born. It was the first network marketing community on the internet. The first day, there were three of us there wondering what to do next. We shared our stories, challenges and insights related to network marketing. Soon there were 10 of us, then 25, then 50, then 100… and then 100's. Networkers from all over the world joined, representing many different companies, happy to find one another, to bond, encourage and exchange ideas.

A few months in, one of the members posted a story that she'd read in a publication called *Upline Magazine*. Follow-up messages poured in from people asking about the publication. There were very few generic network marketing resources, so this was a purple cow for all of us! Since there was no "world wide web" at the time, there was no website. The best she could do was give us their address: 109 W. Water St, Charlottesville, VA 22902.

I stared at the green letters on that monochrome monitor. Blinked. Rubbed my eyes. I wanted to make sure I hadn't fallen asleep and simply dreamt up that address. Charlottesville, Virginia? That's where the University of Virginia was based, and I lived just a few blocks from Water Street!

At the end of my shift, I grabbed breakfast and walked directly to the office. I knocked on the front door. No answer. I knocked harder and the wooden door creaked open. I pushed the door open, "Hello?" Still nothing.

Then I heard some voices at the top of the wooden stairs. I walked in and called upstairs, "Hello?" A girl popped her head down and looked at me with a smile.

"Is the owner here?" I asked.

"Sure. C'mon up! John…? John? Someone's here to see you."

I walked upstairs into the tiny customer service area, two girls happily chatted with customers over the phone. A long-haired fellow approached me and in a deep, gruff voice said, "Hi. I'm John Milton Fogg. Author. Co-founder of *Upline*. And busy. How can I help you?"

I asked for a job, one that was preferably not from midnight to 8 a.m. For some strange reason, he agreed, and that was the start to a life-long friendship. I took home and devoured every issue of *Upline* I could find; along with every book and audio tape that they sold in their 'direct mail catalog.'

To start, I was put in the shipping department, then moved to customer service. As *Upline* grew, I became head of the customer service department where I had the privilege of creating friendships with our customers who were some of the most amazing networkers in the world. Under the mentorship of John Fogg, John David Mann and Randolph Byrd, I worked on catalogs, copy writing, warehousing, sales, and strategy. I traveled to different network marketing company events to represent Upline, making great friends at every stop.

We even hosted events, called The Upline Masters. This was a chance for networkers to travel to one location for several days and learn from some of the Greatest Networkers in the World. It was at one of these events where I met Donna Johnson for the first time. Inspiring. Motivated. Impactful. A proven leader running a massive network marketing organization.

I met Tom "Big Al" Schreiter there as well. Much later, I went on the road with Tom for a few weeks, and there in Arizona, sitting in the front row of a "Big Al's workshop," was Jordan Adler. We actually recorded our first interview right there! Jordan. Humble. Real. Sitting in the front row, always seeking to learn more. A legend.

Then a crazy group of three Norwegians showed up one year. They were on fire! One was a new friend of mine, Orjan Saele. He went on to build one of the largest network marketing organizations in Scandinavia, blazing a trail of growth that had never been seen there before. Innovative. Passionate. Driven. Always asking questions. Orjan ended up being the best man at my wedding. Funny how things work.

One year, Orjan and I were in Thailand for a leadership event when I met with a real-life "sponsor monster" — Mr. Ken Dunn. He was blazing a trail across Asia at the time and happened to have a few days off while we were in Thailand. So we ate, discussed business and swam in the warm waters of the Gulf of Siam. Ken's appetite for creating success is insatiable. It inspires. And he gets things done in record time.

When the Upline Masters events faded away, there was a void in the profession. Network marketers no longer had a place to gather, learn from each other, and celebrate their great profession. I imagined a gathering created by networkers, for networkers... with the primary purpose of "paying it forward."

Could there be an event where the top leaders from different companies would be willing to share the stage and their insights? No agenda, simply paying it forward. The profession had been a blessing to them, and now they could multiply the blessing for others, regardless of what company anyone in the audience had chosen to call their own.

Nearly all professions have an annual gathering or convention, from doctors, to attorneys, to bloggers, etc. Yet network marketers didn't. So we created one by working with presenters who all embraced the vision, chose to be pioneers and showed the world what's possible.

In October of 2003, we put on the first Network Marketing Mastermind Event, and have hosted seven since. The results have been dramatic. Did it work? You bet it did! Thousands of distributors from hundreds of different companies and over 125 countries have attended.

Rock star presenters from different companies not only shared the stage, their knowledge, passion and energy, but they also started to develop friendships, hang out, learn, inspire and even vacation together. We've had dozens of amazing faculty members... people whom I consider revolutionaries, visionaries, dream chasers, innovators, collaborators, and Go-Givers. Each one embraces the concept of building up our profession, instead of allowing inner drama to bring it down.

In November of 2011, my wife Ann and I enjoyed an incredible catamaran adventure in the British Virgin Islands with some great friends, including Mastermind Event presenters Jordan Adler, Donna Johnson, Orjan Saele and Ken Dunn. The catamaran crews took us wherever we wanted, whenever we wanted... from historic Treasure Island to the famous network marketing landmark Peter Island. The food, friendship, memories and conversation were priceless.

One evening while on the beach, Orjan, Donna, Jordan and Ken began discussing the importance of learning how and why to 're-start' someone in the business, and how this can help increase the retention of your organization. After all, we do two things: build an organization and then bond it together. Being able to successfully help someone 'restart' when they've mentally 'quit' builds the organization larger and bonds them to the team.

Some of you may remember back in the 1990's we had a gray box called a Nintendo. It had two buttons, a power button and reset button. And every once-in-a-while during a game we had to pretend "that didn't just happen," and we hit the… reset button! Restart. Well, what if you could simply hit the 'reset' button in your business or help someone on your team restart their business?

That conversation on the beach was the origin of this book, *MLM Heart Attack*. The book is filled with ideas, strategies, techniques, and philosophies from all four of them… and it's all presented as an impactful and entertaining story.

The book also represents what's possible. It's the first book written by four top leaders in our profession, where each leader is in a different network marketing company. A collaboration. A mastermind effect, where multiple minds together create a greater and more powerful mind.

During that catamaran trip, after spending the day swimming and exploring the islands, we'd relax on the deck and watch how the tide coming in raised every ship together, not just our own. It paralleled perfectly with the tide we were all building to raise one another. Each leader built a friendship with the others, fully embracing the idea that you don't win by dragging down your competition; you win by raising up your team… and even further, by raising up our profession of Network Marketing. A rising tide lifts all ships.

Throughout my entire network marketing journey, from the first bulletin board to this collaborative book, my experiences have shown that conflict within this profession is unnecessary. Each step of the way, I saw the natural inclination for leaders in different companies to want to connect with each other, to create a supportive community of success. With all its inherent benefits, Network Marketing as a profession is already incredibly enticing — but when the outside world sees us all getting along, then our profession becomes simply irresistible!

As network marketing professionals, together we can do more to give people their dreams back than all of the government programs combined. We can help rebuild and re-energize the free enterprise system from the ground up — one individual at a time.

But to do this, we're going to have to start a revolution. We have to change the way our business is done. We have to educate our teams better and challenge ourselves to higher levels of leadership. We have to lead with the mantra of "friendship first." And we have to show the world that, regardless of what team we are on, we support each other's dreams.

So, I encourage you and your friends to be part of the growing Revolution!

Dream BIG!

— Art Jonak

Restart the Heart and Your Dreams!

TABLE OF CONTENTS

ONE

Shots Fired

The neon-red clock on the dashboard read: 4:37. It was beginning to sprinkle that early Saturday morning — a day that would change Kurt Dungy's life forever.

The fast-paced, high-pitched squeal from the emergency rescue vehicle blurted out like a locomotive horn as it sped through a stop sign roaming down the two-lane side street, and then suddenly the vehicle rocked as it made a quick left turn onto the four-lane road in the south-west region of Chicago. With red lights flashing, the EMT driver turned on the siren as the engine roared in a high-speed race to Roseland Community Hospital.

Between the hard left jerk and the screeching siren sounds, it caused Kurt to regain consciousness. At first, the bright overhead lights in the ambulance blinded Kurt's vision. He was trying to figure out what happened and where he was. Just then, he saw movement out of the corner of his eyes . . . it was one of the medics working on him. They made direct eye contact.

"Officer Dungy . . . can you hear me?" the medic asked.

Kurt tried desperately to answer. His pulse was weak and when he tried to answer the medic, he realized he couldn't speak. The mild paralysis and his inability to respond naturally freaked Kurt out. He was confused and scared. He closed his eyes trying to recall what the last thing he could remember was.

He could hear the paramedics talking one to another and the siren in the background when he comprehended where in the world he was . . . he was lying on his back, riding in an ambulance. At first, he panicked. Ten years earlier his partner was shot and killed in the line of duty. That dramatic event troubled Kurt so much that for weeks after the incident, he had vivid nightmares of being shot himself.

Kurt was trying to discern if what was happening was a dream or not. Just then they hit a pothole, which caused the ambulance to shake hard. Kurt knew then he wasn't dreaming.

Backtracking his steps in his mind, he started to recall the events from the night. He remembered being in the patrol car with his partner . . . responding to a robbery . . . running — he remembered that he was chasing someone down a dark alley, but it was all a blur.

Kurt closed his eyes trying to remember more when the medic raised his voice and started to talk to him.

"Officer Dungy . . . can you hear me?"

Kurt opened his eyes briefly to let the medic know he could hear him.

"Stay with me," . . . the medic said. . . "Stay with me! We're on our way to the hospital."

Kurt closed his eyes in an attempt to get his bearings and then started to lose consciousness again. Unconscious and unable to respond to the medics, Kurt could still hear the sounds of the siren and, amazingly, he had full recall of his memory.

SEVEN HOURS EARLIER.

Sandy was in the kitchen, putting her finishing touch on Kurt's dinner, which was breakfast — his favorite. The smell of sizzling bacon filled the downstairs as she removed the sunny-side up eggs from the frying pan to Kurt's plate.

"Bryan, tell your dad his dinner's ready," Sandy said to her ten-year-old son, who was lost in his X-box game, so she had to repeat herself to get his attention. . . "Bryan?"

"I'm going," Bryan reluctantly responded as he walked down the long hallway.

Kurt was in the master bathroom, getting ready for his shift. He stared into the mirror . . . still getting used to his "blues."

"Dad, your dinner's ready," Bryan said as he peeked his head around the doorway and then quickly skipped down the hallway to get back to his game.

Kurt walked down the hallway and saw Lorrie in her bedroom on her computer. He paused for a minute and said, "Lorrie, what are you still doing up?"

Lorrie, Kurt's eight-year-old daughter, is the apple of his eye. She is witty, silly, and quick on her feet. Even though Bryan golfed on occasion with Kurt, he still had a soft spot for his little princess.

"I'm updating my profile, what are you doing up?" she replied.

"Very funny . . . it's past your bedtime."

"Dad, it's Friday, and so I don't have school tomorrow," she said proudly.

Kurt still had his days and nights mixed up, and though he tried to hide it, his stress level was building each day.

"I knew that, I was just testing you," he said and then chuckled.

"Right," Lorrie said with a smile.

As Kurt turned to leave . . . Lorrie piped up, "Dad?" Kurt responded with a "what now" look. "Have you thought any more about getting me a cell phone?"

"You'll have to ask your mother."

"But . . . she said 'no'," Lorrie replied with a slight whine in her voice.

"Well, there's your answer," Kurt replied and then quickly ducked away to avoid a "begging session," where he always gives in and then frustrates Sandy.

"But, Dad?"

"Gotta, run . . . late for work," Kurt replied as he walked away abruptly.

He walked into the kitchen, gave Sandy a peck on the cheek. Standing between the table and the granite-top island, Kurt picked up a piece of bacon off the plate that Sandy had prepared, and he started eating.

"Sit down and eat," Sandy insisted in a soft, loving tone.

"Can't, babe," Kurt said with his mouth full. "Gotta watch the pounds," he insisted and then patted his hand on his stomach. "If I get any bigger, this vest won't fit."

Kurt was in reasonable shape. Until the move, he jogged nearly every other day. But he had put on some weight over the past year. Sandy had noticed, but never said anything because Kurt was sensitive about his looks. She could see how the stressful life as a police officer had taken its toll and that he was losing hope in his dream to become financially free. Kurt had set so many goals. He wanted to quit his job eventually, and "the sooner the better" was his model.

It had been six weeks since they moved into the new house, and they still had a few boxes in the garage that needed to be unpacked. Kurt took four weeks' vacation to settle in and two weeks to prepare himself for his new assignment. Sandy knew he was not himself, because Kurt had not put any of the pictures on the fridge.

For several years, Kurt stared at the "cut out" dream pictures on the refrigerator, but when Sandy questioned him about it, he made up the excuse he was still trying to adjust to nights and would get to it when he could. That was not like Kurt.

Kurt, still standing and eating in a hurry, continued to have small talk with Sandy, as he dipped his toast in the runny yolks. "Gotta run hon," Kurt said, chewing the last bite of his breakfast/dinner.

The 6' 2" cop leaned down to kiss his wife, who was a good six inches shorter, when she stopped him with one hand and grabbed a napkin with the other. He had egg yolk in the corner of his mouth, and she was not about to kiss him until it was removed. She smiled and then saw a small drop of egg yolk on his shirt. She wiped his shirt and then his face.

Sandy admired Kurt's work ethic and his desire to take care of his family, but she wished he'd take better care of himself and spend more time with the kids.

They embraced and kissed. "Love you," Kurt said.

"Love you, too," Sandy replied.

Kurt left for work. He had a long drive before he started his shift. Sandy watched him walk out the door. She worried about Kurt. Sure, she never stopped worrying about him being a cop, but instead of the move lifting Kurt's spirits, he seemed more and more discouraged. His excuses seemed legitimate, but he was missing his evening calls with his Multi-level Marketing (MLM) business associates. He had stopped making his calls to prospects, which was totally out of character for Kurt, and he was no longer hanging out with other people in the business.

Sandy had made friends with several of the women in their downline, and the ladies had checked on her since they moved into their new home, but Sandy made up excuses, the move . . . Kurt's new job . . . and transition with the kid's schooling were a way to cover Kurt's recent behavior. Everything seemed legit, so no one thought any different, nor did they know that Kurt's dream was dying. Sandy did, but she didn't want to throw Kurt "under the bus" by revealing the bad habits he was committing. He wasn't eating right or exercising.

Something had to give. Kurt is a strong person, and his job helped him develop a solid work ethic and self-confidence, which were great benefits to his MLM business, but lately he was struggling.

Kurt loved people and loved to have fun. He was always inviting couples and families over for barbeques. He enjoyed helping others, but at times, especially when his downline gave him excuses as to why they weren't working the business, Kurt would go too far, and come across abrasive. Sandy was a good balance for Kurt, and she wasn't afraid to put him in his place when he needed it.

~

It was only Kurt's second week back on patrol. Kurt Dungy was a 15-year veteran of the Chicago Police Department (CPD). In his first 4 years, Kurt served as a patrol officer. In the spring of 2001, he was one of several fellow police officers recruited by Steve Wilkox to work off-duty in security for *The Jerry Springer Show*. Even though Kurt was just trying to make some extra money, Sandy didn't approve of him working there, so he quit.

Two weeks after 9-11, Kurt was promoted to detective and assigned to work undercover in the Organized Crime Division, in narcotics. Three years later, Kurt wanted out of the OC Division, as rumors were flying around that some of the officers from Special Operations Sections (SOS) were being investigated for misconduct. Two of the officers charged were cadets with Kurt in the academy. Five years later, the charges were dropped. But just seven months after that, seven former SOS officers pled guilty to the charges relating to the SOS scandal.

In 2005, Kurt's eighth year on the force, he was one of 70 full-time members who became part of a newly organized SWAT team. He served there for the next six years, until he agreed to move out of the city into the country, in between Southwest Chicago and Crest Hill. That was about the time he started his first attempt at a "part-time" career in network marketing.

The cost of living was getting the best of them, and they were looking for a better school district for the children. And the stress from Kurt's job was getting to him, so Sandy convinced him to move. Eight months prior to the move, Kurt joined his second network marketing business and was excited to get started.

Meanwhile, they found a four-acre lot, with a 2,000 square foot house . . . just perfect, so they thought, with 4 bedrooms and 2.5 baths. However, the 30-mile distance was a 45-minute drive (on a good day) to Morgan Park, Precinct Division 22, where Kurt was recently transferred.

The transit was too far to drive to the SWAT division on the north side of Chicago, so Kurt was back to his original duty, a beat cop. It had been over 10 years since he worked as a street cop, and despite the fact he was a sergeant, District 22 was short-handed, so Kurt had to work nights until his permanent schedule was arranged. Between politics in the ranks and delays in the transfer, Kurt was bound to work the third shift for another month. Sandy dreaded it, but she had been begging Kurt for two years to move out of the suburbs.

Kurt and his new partner, Jim Coleman, had three more hours until their shift ended in Beat 2213, the 22nd District in Southwest Chicago, and Jim hadn't stopped talking since 11 PM. Kurt was tired of explaining his reasoning and logic as to why he and Sandy decided to move out of Chicago proper and into the country. Kurt is athletic, but Jim is a "dyed-in-the-wool" Bears fan, and with the free agent deadline just days away, Jim talked as if he was the GM of an NFL franchise.

"I'm telling ya, for $7.7 million, Forte would be crazy not to accept that contract," Jim said. "And, Bell . . . sure, when Forte went down with his knee injury last year, Bell did a great job filling in, but man, he fumbles too much."

Doesn't this guy ever shut up, Kurt thought to himself as Jim continued to go down the entire roster and give his "two cents" about each starting player. Every now and then, Kurt would nod his head as if he was listening, but he was in another world all together.

Kurt pondered on his former police partner, Mike Shell, who joined the business a few months after Kurt did. Sure, Mike was supportive. He was still tuning in to the 9:30 PM conference calls with Kurt's upline. He knows the plan well. And is always working a prospect, who is just "arm's reach away" from signing up. But in Kurt's eyes, he's pure lazy. Mike's on-again, off-again actions have caused Kurt to keep his distance. The stress has affected their friendship, causing Kurt to doubt his dreams of becoming financially independent and building a sustainable MLM business.

He hated his job, and Jim's non-stop rambling didn't help matters any. Suddenly, Jim was interrupted by a radio request.

"211A in progress," the dispatcher announced. "1200 West 95th Street . . . 10-72."

"That's three blocks down, Kurt. . ." Jim said.

"Light 'em up," he told Jim, as Kurt gripped the wheel tight and pressed the gas pedal to the floor.

Jim grabbed his mic and said, "10-4 . . . Squad 19 responding."

"That's the fourth robbery on 95th this month," Jim said.

Blue lights were flashing, the siren was screaming, and the engine racing, as Kurt drove to the scene. Jim's adrenaline starting pumping as soon as he heard, "10-72," which meant "suspects had a gun."

Kurt and Jim pulled up to a fairly large brick building. "10-97," Jim reported to dispatch that they had arrived at the scene.

As they leaped out of the patrol car, Kurt saw two men dart out a side door. The intruders looked in their direction.

"Stop, Police!" Kurt shouted.

The men took off in opposite directions of each other. Kurt ran south, and Jim went west.

"Suspect is a male . . . black hoodie, dark jeans . . . headed on foot south on Racine Ave. and 96," Kurt shouted into his shoulder microphone as he ran down the sidewalk after the suspect.

Kurt was running with all his might. His daily jogs came in handy now. Just then the robber crossed the street as an oncoming car approached, nearly hitting the man that Kurt was chasing.

"Suspect on foot, headed east down 96th and Genoa Ave," Kurt announced over his radio.

"Move it. . . Move it!" Kurt shouted as he waived at the car, which had stopped abruptly, trying to avoid hitting the criminal. The car stopped in the middle of the road and blocked Kurt's momentum.

Kurt pursued the villain down a narrow dark alley. He could hear the sirens of two other patrol cars arriving. One stopped at the government building where Kurt and Jim left their patrol car, and the other was approaching down Genoa, just one block away.

Meanwhile, Jim was "zooming in" on his assailant. The robber attempted to climb the 10-foot security fence, lost his footing, and fell. Jim quickly apprehended him and pulled out his cuffs when he heard something no cop ever wants to hear in a pursuit. He quickly placed the suspect in the patrol car and began to run.

Kurt had heard the backup squad car give their 10-20, so he knew assistance would arrive any second. Just then, Kurt's legs started to stiffen and his chest tighten. It had been several years since he chased down a suspect. *But I jog regularly*, he thought to himself as he felt his muscles tightening up. Kurt started panting heavily.

Just then, two patrol officers appeared in the distance, about 100 yards ahead of Kurt.

"Stop, Police!" one of the officers screamed.

"Gun!" shouted the other officer.

BAM!

It happened so fast.

"Squad 26 . . . Gotta 10-71 and a 10-53," an officer said to inform that a shooting had occurred and a man was down.

The two officers were wrestling the suspect, when Jim knelt where Kurt was lying.

"Kurt! Kurt!" Jim yelled.

"Are you hit?" he continued.

Kurt lay on the dirty, cold pavement face down and not responding. Jim was afraid to move Kurt, and it was so dark, he couldn't tell if Kurt had been shot or not. He patted Kurt down to be sure he had his vest on.

"Squad 19 . . . I have a code 30 . . . and 11-41. . . Get me a bus, NOW!" Jim shouted with the horror of the situation.

The situation was serious. An ambulance was needed for Kurt and one for the suspect who had just been shot by a responding patrol officer.

Jim knew what to do, but didn't want to do it. He reached down and checked Kurt's pulse on his neck.

"Damn it, Kurt . . . don't you die on me, man!" he said.

TWO

The Ride

Fifteen minutes had passed since the medics loaded Kurt on the stretcher. His vital signs were touch and go. Fortunately, there was little to no traffic at that hour and, with fifteen more minutes to the closest hospital, Kurt was hanging on by a thread.

"His pulse is dropping!" one of the medics declared with urgency.

Kurt could still hear everything that was going on, but was still unable to respond and still wasn't sure what happened. Then he remembered more vividly the sudden pain he felt in his chest. . . *I was running . . . that's right, I was running,* Kurt thought to himself as he reflected back on the incident. He remembered the man with a dark hoodie, and he could see himself racing down the dark alley after him. *Was I shot?* Kurt considered again. The last thing he could recall was a sharp pain in his chest and then hearing one of the backup officers shouting, "Gun!"

At that moment, Kurt had grabbed his chest and fell to the ground. He blacked out and had no recollection as to what happened after that until now.

After Jim arrived on the scene, the call to dispatch went out reporting — "shots fired." The information reported was that one of the suspects was shot, in critical condition, and that an officer was down.

Based on that situation, the calls went to command centers in Morgan Park and Washington Heights, both just four to five minutes away from where Kurt lay. First, Engine 92 and Ambulance 17 arrived, and less than 60 seconds later, Engine 120 and Emergency Units 91 and 21 appeared.

When the emergency vehicles arrived on the scene, there were three patrol cars from District 5. . . three police cars from District 6 . . . and a sheriff's squad car from District 8. Several officers were securing the crime scene while two others were using flashlights, searching for bullet casings on the ground.

Jim was talking to a commanding officer when the medics walked up to where Kurt was lying. He was still face down and unconscious. Three medics went to the suspect, and four medics immediately went to Kurt.

After the medic introduced himself to Jim, he began to ask a series of questions.

"Do you know the injured officer?"

"Yes, he's my partner," Jim replied.

"How well do you know him?"

"Not that well . . . I guess . . . I mean he just got transferred from SWAT division and. . ."

"What's his name?" the medic interrupted.

"Kurt Dungy," Jim answered, as he nervously paced back and forth.

"How old is he?"

Before Jim had a chance to answer, Officer Mike Shell, Kurt's former partner and friend, arrived on the scene and spoke up, "42. . . He's 42 years old."

The Medic turned to Mike, because he seemed more knowledgeable. "Do you know his medical history . . . Does he have any allergies?"

"As far as I know, he has no allergies, and he's in good health. He's a runner, athletic . . . never had surgery. . . As a matter of fact, Kurt ain't ever been in the hospital for anything," Mike replied.

"Can you tell me what happened?" the medic inquired. Jim stepped forward and began to explain what he knew, as did the other two officers who were involved in the shooting and the arrest of the suspect Kurt was chasing.

Meanwhile, the other medics continued to tend to Kurt. They cautiously rolled him over onto his back. There was no sign of blood on Kurt or near his body.

"I have a pulse, but it's faint," said one medic.

A medic leaned down to examine Kurt's eyes. He turned toward the interviewing medic and asked, "What's his name?"

"Kurt," he replied. . . "Kurt Dungy."

"Officer Dungy, can you hear me?" the concerned medic inquired. No response.

The medics quickly began to remove Kurt's shirt by cutting it with medical utility scissors. They removed his protective vest, and there was no sign of any wounds or external injuries.

Another medic went to the medical unit vehicle and retrieved a backboard. He laid the plastic board besides Kurt and, with a gentle push, they log rolled him onto the backboard. One medic strapped him in, as another wheeled the stretcher parallel to Kurt.

"One. . . two. . . three!" The medics lifted Kurt up and positioned him on the stretcher. They strapped Kurt down and wheeled him to the emergency vehicle. Once they got Kurt into the unit, they began working on him.

"Just a few more minutes . . . Hang in there, Kurt," the lead medic said out loud.

Surprisingly, Kurt heard him say, "Hang in there."

"His pulse is still weak," a medic said.

The three medics were working frantically to prepare Kurt for transport. Two patches (about the size of a man's hand) were placed on each side of Kurt's chest. Wires were connected to the patches and hooked up to a monitor. A fingertip monitor that is used to watch blood pressure and heart rate was placed on Kurt's index finger.

One of the medics, with a concerned look on his face, turned to the other two and said, "His SpO2 is 88% and his heart rate is 158."

Kurt was having an MLM heart attack. His oxygen saturation level was in jeopardy, and his heart was racing full speed with spasms.

Jim and Mike walked up to the back of the emergency unit vehicle and peeked through the window as the three medics were busy working on Kurt.

The fourth medic, who was also the driver, walked up to the concerned officers. "Can I help you, officers?"

"What's going on?" Mike asked.

"We're doing everything we can," the medic replied.

"What's wrong with him?" Jim inquired.

Recognizing the situation was serious, Jeremiah, one of the medics in the EUV, spontaneously took the lead. He started barking out orders, and his trained associates were with him all the way, working together to save Kurt's life. They needed to act fast and act now.

"BP?" Jeremiah asked.

"BP . . . Dropping," said one of the medics.

"Okay, we gotta V-Fib."

Pointing to the IV package, Jeremiah instructed, "Get me a line." To the other, he said, "Start an MVB. I'll start compression."

Kurt's blood pressure (BP) was dropping rapidly. Things deteriorated in a matter of minutes. The lead medic, Jeremiah, pronounced Kurt in a "V-Fib" condition. V-Fib (ventricular fibrillation) is a condition where the ventricles in the heart begin to quiver rather than contract properly. Typically, the human body has approximately five minutes of blood in their body, but it needs to circulate or the patient will die. Kurt's blood is like the dream that remains dormant inside a person. He just needed someone to help him circulate that dream before it was too late.

"Getting a line" is the term used for an IV, so a medic responded swiftly by opening an IV package. He grabbed an IV bag and positioned it on the pole bolted to the interior wall of the emergency vehicle. He bled the line to remove any air. Then, the medic tied a tourniquet (that looks like a large rubber band) around his bicep. Instantly, Kurt's veins enlarged, making it easy to find a superior vein in his arm. Next, he inserted an 18-gauge needle into his forearm and a small drop of blood perfused. Then, the medic injected the catheter, connected the line, and started the IV.

"I got an 18-gauge in his right AC," the medic said to Jeremiah.

At the same time, another medic started a manual ventilation bag (MVB). Kurt had stopped breathing.

Just then, Jeremiah stood up and stooped directly over the top of Kurt. He placed his right hand in the middle of his chest, overlapped and interlocked his left hand, and began CPR. He pushed hard and fast. The cartilage around Kurt's rib cage cracked with each thrust from the first series of three compressions. It sounded like a twig snapping each time Jeremiah pushed down on Kurt's chest, and after a few seconds, the sound effects stopped. To a novice, it would appear that a person's ribs were cracking, but to a trained medic, it was normal and part of the training.

For two minutes, Kurt received roughly 100 chest compressions and approximately twenty bursts of air. Jeremiah stopped performing CPR, and they waited to see how Kurt would respond. They checked their watches to count down two minutes, hoping for Kurt's body to respond.

With his wrist upright, staring at his watch, a medic replied, "Two minutes."

"Check pulse," Jeremiah asked.

"No pulse," the other responded.

"Check rhythm."

The medic looked at Jeremiah and shook his head from left to right. Kurt was not responding to the CPR.

Jeremiah looked at the medic who prepared the IV and said, "Get ready to charge 360 joules!"

Jeremiah started the chest compressions again, while the medic examined the electrode pad patches on Kurt chest and side. They had no choice. The next step to save Kurt's life was defibrillation (an electric charge to the heart). When a person has a severe heart attack, the heart goes into spasms and the rhythm is irregular, racing so fast that it burns up, and quits.

A medic instigated a charge, and the sound of the mechanism echoed like a train whistle, getting louder by the second. In 6 seconds, the monitor screen read: "Ready to Deliver Shock."

"Okay, ready to shock!" said the medic.

"Clear patient . . . Clear!" Jeremiah shouted.

The medic pressed the button, and 360 joules of electric current shot through the lines and into the electrode pads. Kurt's body leaped upward and jolted from the electric current.

The monitor screen read, "Shock delivered."

"MVB!" Jeremiah instructed as he climbed back up on top of Kurt and continued with chest compressions. The medic resumed the manual ventilation, and another examined the fingertip monitor and checked the IV.

Jeremiah was panting now as he continued chest compressions. Winded and out of breath he asked again, "Rhythm?"

The medic shakes his head.

"Pulse?" Jeremiah inquired.

Again, the medic shakes his head in defeat and says, "No pulse."

"Asystole!" Jeremiah exclaimed. Kurt's heart showed no electrical activity, and he had flatlined. Immediately, Jeremiah climbed back up and over Kurt and began CPR.

Jeremiah was 28 years old, and he had only been in this predicament once before. He was top of his class and outscored over 102 applicants to get his job. It was his fifth year as a medic, but he never had anyone die on his watch before, and he wasn't about to let it happen to Kurt.

With force and tenacity, Jeremiah was regretting the situation. It was his night off, and he had agreed to switch with someone else at his station. *I'm not supposed to be here*, Jeremiah thought to himself, as he continued to perform CPR. Repeatedly, he thrust up and down — pushing with each compression, saying, "Not on my watch." He paused for a couple of seconds to catch his breath.

"Need a break?" one of the medics asked Jeremiah.

"Nah. . . I'll be all right," he said with determination.

He looked into Kurt's face, and he thought about his dad. Kurt was just a few years younger than his father was. Every week Jeremiah's father called him to ask about his runs. Jeremiah thought about what he was going to say to his dad when he called that weekend.

It was time to start compressions again. The distance to the hospital was about twenty to twenty-five minutes, and because it was about 5:00 AM, traffic was minimal, and they were making good time. Jeremiah started doing the chest compressions again.

Suddenly, Jeremiah pictured himself talking to his dad on the phone the next day, telling his father about this ambulance ride . . . how he wasn't supposed to be here, and that this was his first critical run where he was the lead medic. And he imagined himself saying, "Dad, it's like this guy was having an MLM heart attack, and he needed me and my guys to revive him."

Each time Jeremiah pushed down on Kurt's chest, his body jerked with movement.

For a second time Kurt opened his eyes! When he did, Jeremiah stopped performing CPR. He had been giving him CPR, off and on, for five minutes or more. Obviously, given the situation, the medics were quite surprised that he opened his eyes.

"Kurt, I don't know if you can hear me," Jeremiah said. "We are two minutes away from the hospital. . . There's a team of doctors waiting for us."

Just then, Kurt's eyes turned and stopped, looking directly into Jeremiah's eyes. His vitals starting improving, and his pulse was steadily rising. Kurt wasn't out of the woods yet, but it was a good sign he was going to make it.

Confidently, the medic continued, "You've had an MLM heart attack . . . but don't you worry, you're in good hands. This hospital has one of the best cardiac care units in the world."

THREE

The Notification

They arrived at the hospital. The driver opened the double doors and said, "All right boys, let's get him inside."

The rainfall increased as they wheeled Kurt up the ramp. The emergency doors to the hospital opened automatically as they guided the stretcher inside. The emergency entryway was filled with five doctors and approximately seven nurses standing by and waiting for Kurt's arrival. Immediately, Kurt was rushed to the trauma center and the typical hospital care commotion began.

One of the medics was rambling off Kurt's vital signs, "blood pressure 165 over 110, temperature 98, pulse 60, SpO2 90% and heart rate 152." Jeremiah gave a brief overview of the procedures they performed in the ambulance to Dr. Jack McCarthy.

Dr. McCarthy was a huge sports fan, and when Michael Jordan played basketball for the Chicago Bulls he had season tickets. Unfortunately, he was in residency and didn't get to see as many games as he wished. But because of his love for the game and his obsession for Michael Jordan, his colleagues and cardiac residents nicknamed him, "Dr. J," and it had stuck with him ever since.

Jeremiah had met Dr. J before and heard that he was one of the leading heart surgeons in Chicago and was well-liked by others in the medical field. Dr. J was 55 years old, bald (by choice), and well spoken of by his colleagues because he was positive, soft-spoken, thoughtful, and kind to his patients.

After giving his report to Dr. J, he asked Jeremiah to repeat his steps; after all, only five minutes earlier Kurt had flatlined. But when he came into the hospital, everything changed. He was still weak, but stable. Dr. J stepped into a side room in the trauma center to discuss Kurt's initial diagnosis. So, as the lead medic, he gave a "play-by-play" of Kurt's condition and the treatment applied before arriving at the hospital.

Dr. J is one of several cardiac surgeons at Roseland Community, and is considered the best in his field, specializing in MLM heart attacks. Dr. J and Jeremiah finished their conversation concerning Kurt, and the medic went on his way as Dr. J gave directions to the nursing staff.

Kurt was immediately taken to the trauma center to get a diagnosis of his heart condition. The nurses compared his current vitals, pulse rate, blood pressure, respiration rate and temperature with that given by the rescue unit. An EKG was scheduled, while a new intravenous line was placed and oxygen started . . . then blood work drawn and sent to the lab. While Kurt's tests were pending, he lay completely exhausted. Then the hospital personnel moved Kurt from the emergency trauma center to ICU. Dr. J would become his MLM heart specialist.

~

Meanwhile, Lieutenant Parker, Kurt's regional supervisor, who was the commanding officer on the scene, followed police protocol and contacted Chicago's chief of police to inform him of Kurt's condition and get directions for organizing the Notification Team that would go to Kurt's home and notify Sandy. The officers on the scene were concerned about Kurt's condition and shocked that he had had a heart attack.

The chief appointed Captain Frank Lugo to be the lead officer of the Notification Team. Lugo lived on the southwest side of Chicago and was a ranking officer who had handled several family notifications in his lengthy career. Even though Officer Mike Shell was only a patrol officer, he was also appointed to accompany Captain Lugo because he was closest to the family. An additional patrol car followed to drive Sandy to the hospital. It was important to reach Sandy as soon as possible because Kurt was non-responsive, and no one knew Kurt's medical history but her. In order to get an immediate diagnosis, Sandy's input was vital. Even though he was semi-conscious, Kurt had just flatlined, was in critical condition and in intensive care.

The ride to Kurt's residence seemed to take forever, partly because of the distance to his country home, a good thirty minutes from the outskirts of Chicago, and also because Mike's anxiety level was high. He knew that he had to inform Sandy. As he rode with Captain Lugo, Mike sat silent, almost numb, as he stared into the blackness, hypnotized by the grinding windshield wipers as they motioned up and down against the glass. This was Mike's first time notifying a family member, and he repeatedly imagined Sandy's response in his mind.

He had been to Kurt's previous house multiple times over the past few months for team meetings. Kurt sponsored Mike in the business. In fact, Mike was Kurt's first prospect. The days of excitement at Kurt's house had gradually faded away. Gazing through the passenger window, he could see the dash lights and Captain Lugo's reflection. But as he reminisced of the meetings at Kurt's house . . . the special times they had when key leaders from the business visited Kurt's home . . . Mike's mind was far away from the patrol car.

What amazing times, Mike thought. He recalled one meeting, *what a crowd*. Mike could see Kurt's house, it was packed wall-to-wall, there were people sitting everywhere, on the steps, on the floor, even on the kitchen counter. It was as if it were yesterday. He could still remember the keynote speaker saying, "Never put off to tomorrow what you can do today." The enthusiasm that night was electric.

"You are the sum total of the five people you spend the most time with," the speaker said. . . "Who you spend your time with will determine your success." Mike regretted not putting more effort into the business. As he thought of Kurt, he wondered if he might be part of the cause of Kurt's condition. After all, he avoided Kurt's phone calls many times, and when he promised Kurt he would be at a meeting, he was a "no show."

"My goodness, Dungy lives out in the sticks," Captain Lugo said.

The Captain's statement was the first word he had spoke in over twenty minutes, so it not only startled Mike, it caught him off guard, as he daydreamed of the speaker's motivational talk at Kurt's house.

Mike had never been to Kurt's new home, and the ride did seem to take an "eternity" to get there, so to appear that he was focused on the notification and not thinking about network marketing . . . Mike quickly agreed with a seemingly natural response, "For real!"

~

The doorbell rings.

Half asleep and hardly attentive, the ring can barely be heard because the master bedroom is nestled in the far back of the ranch-style home.

The doorbell rang again.

Sandy passively rolls over, wondering if the doorbell was from her dream or not. She wraps her arms around Kurt's pillow, pulling it close and squeezing it tight.

Captain Lugo pressed the doorbell a third time.

"She's probably sleeping," Mike said.

Captain Lugo looked at Mike, "Ya think?" He pushed it again.

Sandy opened her eyes but just laid there a moment longer when the doorbell rang again. *Is someone at the door?* she thought.

Then suddenly it hit her. "Kurt," she shouted aloud as she sat straight up, throwing the bed covers off her upper torso. "Oh, my God!" she said in a panic as she turned to see what time it was. It was 5:27 AM.

The Dungy's had only lived there a few weeks, and no immediate family member had visited yet. Sandy's mother had discussed coming for Easter break to see Bryan and Lorrie. But that didn't explain why someone would be at her door this early. Sandy was already thinking the worst before she even got out of the bed. For her, it was something she had thought about many times but hoped that she would never have to face it.

31

Sandy jumped out of bed and rushed down the hallway as she hurriedly tied the sash of her nightgown. She flipped the light switch in the foyer. The streetlight in the front yard cast a dark silhouette of two men standing at the front door. She turned the front porch light on and could see two police officers in their "blues" . . . her fears were correct, *oh no*, she thought to herself. She took a deep breath, unlocked the deadbolt, gripped the door handle and opened the door.

"Mrs. Dungy, I'm Captain Frank Lugo and this is Officer Mike Shell."

It had been about six months since Mike was last in Kurt and Sandy's home. But between the adrenaline rush and Mike's police cap, she didn't recognize him at first. She just stood there. Sandy stared at Mike's star . . . as Chicago's police department refers to it, instead of the typical badge. Mike's five-pointed star-shaped badge was silver-colored metal, with broad points. Sandy remembered looking at Kurt's star the night before, when she wiped the egg yolk from his shirt and mouth.

"May we come in?" Captain Lugo said in a professional but gentle voice.

Trying her best to hold her composure, Sandy invited them in and shut the door behind them.

Captain Lugo removed his hat, as did Mike. Holding it with two hands, the Captain pointed it toward the couch and said, "Mrs. Dungy, please . . . take a seat."

She sat down first and then the officers followed. Captain Lugo explained the situation and was straight forward . . . "He's in critical condition." Sandy seemed to be taking it well. After about fifteen minutes of going over the procedures to get Sandy to the hospital and to provide childcare for the children, she dismissed herself to get dressed and ride with the officers to the hospital.

By now, Bryan had made his way to the kitchen. He saw the officers in the living room and immediately hugged his mom. She encouraged him that everything was going to be all right. Mike was moved emotionally when he saw Sandy hug Bryan . . . and that was when he noticed the refrigerator. There were no vision pictures. Kurt always had his "dream" pictures on his refrigerator. He kept his "yet-to-be-fulfilled" vision pictures on his fridge side and the "accomplished" ones on his freezer side. Mike realized it was worse than what he originally thought; Kurt was not taking care of himself.

Sandy reentered the living room. Her neighbor, Mary, had already arrived. Mary had two children the same age as Bryan and Lorrie. She and Sandy took turns driving the children to school and had spent a few afternoons chatting about the local PTA.

Mary immediately hugged Sandy.

"Thank you so much, Mary," Sandy said.

"It's not a problem; I'm just glad I could help," she answered.

Sandy looked at Captain Lugo. "I'm ready now."

"The officers are in the driveway, ready to take you to the hospital," the Captain replied.

Sandy walked toward the door and turned around. "Mary, I'll call you as soon as I know more."

"Let me know what I can do . . . if you need me to, I can bring Bryan and Lorrie to the hospital."

One of the officers got out of the patrol car and opened the back door for Sandy as she walked down the driveway. Sandy got in, he shut the door, and they drove off to the hospital.

FOUR

Dr. J

The sound from a nurse in the room, who was resetting the IV machine, woke Kurt. He could feel the oxygen tube in his nose and the IV in his right arm. He looked down and saw cords running down his hospital gown. When he went to get a better look at the cardiology lines, he quickly stopped leaning forward because of the sharp pain he felt in his chest.

"What happened?" Kurt said in a soft tone.

The nurse had her back to Kurt. Surprised to hear him speak, she turned around abruptly.

"Mr. Dungy . . . you're awake," she replied.

Kurt cleared his throat, "I'm thirsty."

"You'll need to wait until Dr. McCarthy comes and speaks with you. He's reading your charts now and will be right in."

She walked out of his 10' x 10' intensive care room and pulled the door, leaving it only about an inch open.

"He's awake," the nurse said to Dr. McCarthy, who was standing by the ICU desk reading Kurt's chart.

"Is he? . . . Why, that's a good sign," he said.

About three or four minutes went by, and then Dr. McCarthy entered Kurt's room. Kurt had already fallen back asleep.

"Mr. Dungy?"

Kurt opened his eyes.

"Mr. Dungy . . . my name is Dr. Jack McCarthy . . . but everyone calls me Dr. J. I'm a cardiologist, and I will be taking care of you. How do you feel?"

"Like a Mack truck ran over me," Kurt said. "What happened?"

"You've had an MLM heart attack," Dr. J replied.

Kurt turned his head and looked at Dr. McCarthy with a puzzled look on his face. "If I've had an MLM heart attack, why do my ribs hurt so bad?"

"Well, Mr. Dungy . . . while en route to the hospital this morning, the medics had to perform over five hundred chest impressions to keep you alive — you flatlined."

"What?" Kurt responded.

"That's right, you flatlined," Dr. McCarthy answered nonchalantly as he looked at Kurt's charts and appeared to be scanning over them. "So that's the Mack truck feeling you're referring to."

"Where's my wife?" Kurt asked.

"My understanding is she is being escorted by some of your coworkers on the force; she should be here shortly," Dr. McCarthy replied.

It started to sink in . . . an MLM heart attack. Kurt started to rehearse in his mind what had happened. As for the last two hours, it was mostly a blur; but as for the past six months, Kurt knew exactly what he had NOT done, which, no doubt, was what had put him in intensive care. He had lost momentum and neglected to stay true to the health of his business.

"Do you realize how fortunate you are?" Dr. McCarthy asked Kurt. "Many patients, whose hearts have stopped, don't restart. The medics had to revive your heart."

Kurt just lay there silent.

"When you came in, your vitals were very low. Your success meter shows a poor performance record and a lack of self-confidence. That's not good, and it concerns me . . . it's one of the reasons why you are here. It appears that you have had a lack of success signing people up or keeping them. Which is it, Kurt?"

"Both . . . but more of the latter, I guess." Kurt replied.

"How you view success is important to remain healthy."

Kurt was rather surprised as to Dr. McCarthy's knowledge.

"I'm going to need to ask you a few questions to discover what's been going on and to better diagnosis your condition," Dr. McCarthy said.

"Okay," Kurt replied.

Dr. McCarthy looked at his clipboard again and started right in. "According to the police report, you collapsed while in pursuit of a suspect . . . an alleged robbery. Do you remember that?"

Kurt thought for a second, "Yes, I remember responding to a 211A in progress."

"When did you first start feeling chest pain?" the doctor asked.

"Actually . . . in the patrol car, sometime around 4 AM. I was feeling pretty down."

"And did anything happen to bring that on?"

"Yes," Kurt said affirmatively.

"And what was that?"

"My partner, he was driving me crazy. The more he talked the more I felt stressed." Kurt watched as Dr. McCarthy lifted his eyes. His reading eyeglasses were halfway down his nose and he looked over the top of them to stare at Kurt.

"No, I'm serious . . . wait, it wasn't actually my partner per se, it's the way I feel when I get around people like him . . . you know, negative."

"I see. Do you have any other health problems?"

"Yes, doubts and distractions. . ."

"Severe?"

"Very," Kurt admitted.

"What about bad habits?" Dr. McCarthy asked.

"I'm embarrassed to say."

"There's nothing to be embarrassed about; I'm here to help you, not criticize you," Dr. J reassured.

"Somehow, I lost my urgency. My wife wanted to move out to the country, and I didn't want to do it. It was causing us stress and I started complaining about it, thinking negatively about it. Before I knew it, I was figuring that once we moved, I would live so far out of the city that no one would come to my house for a presentation. So I figured, what's the use; I may as well quit now and save myself the agony of defeat."

"I see," Dr. J affirmed.

"I'm a cop," Kurt said. "My job takes so much of my time, I'm on nights now, and I don't have time to make calls."

"How long have you been experiencing these obstacles?"

"I thought I was getting better," Kurt answered.

"What do you mean?" Dr. J asked.

"A few years ago, I was first introduced to a business, and I started out strong. But everyone had heard of that company, and I quickly ran out of people to talk to — someone else had already approached them. Everywhere I turned, people did not want to hear about it. As soon as I mentioned I had a business opportunity I wanted to share with them, they quickly mentioned the name of the company and turned me off like a light switch. They all said the products were too expensive. Besides, I was in the SWAT division, and my schedule prohibited me from getting time off to go to the events. So, eventually, I quit."

"Go on," the doctor said.

"Then about ten months ago, I found a new company. I was so excited, no one had heard of it, so in my mind I felt it would be easier to convince people to come to my house. My sponsor's upline is really successful, and he came to my home several times. We even had a special speaker come in from Canada. He was awesome. People were signing up . . . left and right."

"What happened then?"

"I had over 20 people join in two weeks. Then it happened. Family members and friends started to steal the dream from my downline and 15 out of the 20 people I sponsored fizzled out within three months. It was so disappointing. So I went to a convention and got really fired up again. I worked the business with a new zeal. The following month, 12 more people joined the business. But, once again, my work schedule prevented me from staying in touch, and they too dropped out."

"Sounds like you've had some severe obstacles clogging your arteries."

"You can say that again," Kurt said.

"You know, Kurt, every person has obstacles, but if you don't treat them, it will worsen your condition and eventually take you out." Dr. J said.

"That's for sure," Kurt agreed.

"But here's the catch. In your case, your obstacles have become bigger than your dream," Dr. McCarthy said as he laid his clipboard down on a small table next to Kurt's bed.

"Kurt, let me ask you . . . you are a police officer," Dr. J paused for a second, "Is that your dream?"

"No, I hate my job," Kurt replied.

"So, it's safe to say then, you started a networking business because you wanted something different in life, correct?"

"Yes, the money is good, but the hours . . ." Kurt answered. "I mean . . . I never get to see my kids." Kurt paused a moment, "I really thought that I could do it part-time and then earn enough over a couple of years to leave my job and do the business full-time. At least that was my goal. But now look at me."

"Kurt, do you want to continue with your career as a police officer?" Dr. J asked.

"No, I want so much more."

"How much would it take for you to quit your job?"

"Well, I make $3,000 a month now. . ."

"What if you were making $5,000 a month, would that excite you?"

"Absolutely!" Kurt replied.

"Well what we need to do is get a proper diagnosis and get you started back on track for your dream."

"That's what I want," Kurt answered.

"Once you understand the power of CPR, you will begin to resuscitate the dream."

"CPR hurts, if you ask me," Kurt smirked.

"Not if you get the right CPR. In order to prevent an MLM heart attack, you need to define CPR correctly. "C" stands for *Culture* and

Community. "P" stands for *Prospecting* and *Products.* "R" stands for *Repetition* and *Relationships.*"

Dr. McCarthy informed Kurt that a few more tests were necessary to determine how much damage the MLM heart attack had affected his health, and after that, he would give him more information.

~

The patrol car that provided Sandy an escort to the hospital arrived at 7:19 AM. The two police officers walked with Sandy to the emergency area. A nurse was waiting at the front desk and instructed them where to go.

The three of them walked down the hall and stopped at the elevator. One of the officers pressed the "up" button. The door opened. They entered. Sandy stepped forward and pushed "L-3." The door shut. Sandy stood lifeless as she listened to motorized pulleys that motioned the elevator to the third floor. She still did not have any details as to Kurt's condition. She mentally prepared herself for the worst as she pictured Kurt lying in a hospital bed. Her mind wandered concerning their future, finances, and the kids. Fear gripped her heart as the elevator doors opened, then she and the two officers exited together.

The sign on the wall directed her to turn left and go down the hallway to ICU. Sandy proceeded down a narrow white hallway as the sound of the officers' boots echoed each time they clapped on the tile floor. The smell of chemicals and the stench of body odor created a sense of reality. . . Kurt was in the hospital — it wasn't a dream, but a reality.

"Hi, I'm Sandy Dungy. . . My husband is Kurt Dungy . . . he was just admitted. What room, please?" she said to the nurse seated behind a massive desk lined with medical monitors.

One of the nurses behind the desk stepped forward, "Come with me, Mrs. Dungy."

"We'll wait here for you, ma'am . . . let us know if there is anything we can do," one of the officers said.

"Thank you," Sandy replied as she turned and followed the nurse in the opposite direction.

The nurse proceeded and pressed a button on the wall. The large door to the ICU opened automatically. She escorted Sandy to the ICU station. As she entered the large Intensive Care area, the sounds of the medical equipment resonated in the sterile background and sounded extremely loud, which magnified her anticipation.

"Wait here," the nurse said. "I'll get the doctor for you."

"Okay, thank you," Sandy replied.

Fear of the unknown kept Sandy anxious as she patiently waited for the doctor to come and speak with her. She gazed around the ICU, wondering which room was Kurt's. All the rooms had large glass windows, although the majority of them had curtains that enclosed the room preventing a person from viewing inside.

Once again, Sandy attempted to prepare herself for what she was about to face. She, too, like Kurt, recalled the emotions that followed when Kurt's former partner was shot and killed in years past. All she could think of was, *what am I going to tell the kids?*

Just then, the nurse returned from around the corner with Dr. McCarthy. His humble appearance and pleasant smile eased her emotions as he approached.

"Dr. McCarthy, this is Mrs. Dungy, Kurt's wife," the nurse cordially introduced Kurt's attending physician.

"Call me Sandy," she insisted.

"Sandy, my name is Dr. McCarthy; I am Kurt's cardiologist. You can call me Dr. J."

Sandy was not familiar with basketball, so she had no idea what "Dr. J" meant, so she continued with her greeting. "Nice to meet you," Sandy said as Dr. McCarthy reached out his hand for a gentle greeting. They shook hands.

"When can I see my husband?" she asked.

"In one moment . . . he's resting peacefully," Dr. McCarthy said.

Those words brought such comfort; it felt like a heavy load was released from Sandy, and she smiled cautiously.

"Is he all right?" she asked.

"We're still doing tests, which will help determine how much damage there is to his heart, but he was able to communicate clearly with me a few minutes ago, and besides being sore, he seems to be doing fairly well, considering. . ."

"Considering?" Sandy questioned.

"Yes, considering he has suffered a massive heart attack."

"A heart attack?" she asked.

"Yes, Kurt has suffered an MLM heart attack. He flatlined in the ambulance, and medics performed CPR. They were able to resuscitate him," Dr. McCarthy said pointedly to Sandy.

"Oh my gosh," Sandy gasped.

"Does MLM heart disease run in your family?" Dr. McCarthy probed.

"No, to my knowledge, no one in Kurt's family has experienced network marketing," Sandy said.

"What about health problems; has Kurt suffered from any doubts or disappointments?" he added.

"Yes, over the past few weeks and months, he has had several setbacks and obstacles."

"Is he currently on any upline medication?"

"No, he's refused to take any."

"I see," Dr. McCarthy said as he penned down Sandy's answers.

"What about habits? Does he watch excessive television, forgo to make prospect calls, or has Kurt missed any weekly team conference calls?"

"Yes, all of the above," she replied.

"Has Kurt experienced any risk factors . . . such as dream stealing or retention loss?"

"He's been mocked in the locker room at work," Sandy admitted.

"I see," Dr. McCarthy responded.

"Risk factors, some, yes, but more with his downline . . . that has really caused some unusual health problems," Sandy said.

"Such as?" Dr. McCarthy asked.

"Well, I'm not a doctor, but I've noticed symptoms of La-Z-Boy arthritis, remote control paralysis, and prospect numbness," Sandy replied.

"Well, I am a doctor, and those symptoms sound about right for someone in Kurt's condition," Dr. McCarthy said with a grin.

Sandy smiled back; she started to feel more at ease.

"Well, this information helps me greatly . . . would you like to see your husband now?" Dr. McCarthy asked.

"Yes, please. . ." Sandy responded.

"Follow me," he replied.

Sandy followed Dr. McCarthy to Kurt's room. The doctor opened the door. The room was filled with several monitors and cardiac equipment. Kurt was sound asleep.

Immediately, Sandy got emotional. She was taken aback as she viewed Kurt lying there with a breathing tube in his nose and medical apparatus down his hospital gown. She approached Kurt and ran her hand gently across his military shaved head. The prickly hairs tickled her hand which caused her to smile and brought a tear to her eye.

"Kurt?" Dr. McCarthy said from the far side of the bed to wake him.

Kurt opened his eyes and looked in the direction of the voice that called his name. He looked directly at Dr. McCarthy.

"There's someone here that would like to say hello," he said.

Kurt turned his head to his left. Before him was his beautiful wife, Sandy.

"Hey, girl," he said with a rasp in his voice.

"If you wanted to get my attention, you didn't need to go to this expense to get it," Sandy said in jest.

Kurt started to chuckle and his laugh quickly turned into moans as he placed his hand over his chest. "That hurts," he said, trying to stop laughing.

"It should; you have two cracked ribs," Dr. McCarthy said.

Sandy turned and looked at Dr. McCarthy with one eyebrow raised as if to say, "*What's that all about?*"

"That's typical with a case like Kurt's. His heart stopped, and he had fifteen minutes of CPR. That would hurt anyone."

Sandy looked back at Kurt with deep sympathy.

"Where are the kids?" Kurt asked Sandy.

"They're with Mary, from down the street. I spoke with her on the phone out in the lobby. She's bringing them . . . they should be here in a half hour or so."

Sandy turned to Dr. McCarthy, "Do you think it would be all right if they saw their dad?" she asked.

"I suppose just for a minute would be fine. . . Kurt is going to need some rest; we will begin analyzing his tests to get a final diagnosis, and then we will begin treatment."

Sandy turned back to Kurt, grabbed his hand and said, "That sounds great."

"Sure does," Kurt agreed.

"The road to recovery isn't overnight, but with the right people in your life, you will be back in business in no time," Dr. McCarthy replied.

Sandy noticed how tired Kurt looked. She had seen the signs of an MLM heart attack, but was too afraid to say anything, lest she make matters worse. *I should have said something before it came to this,* she thought to herself.

The awkward silence caught Sandy off guard as she thought about Kurt's deterioration over the past few months, but then quickly recovered and said, "Great."

Dr. McCarthy looked at Kurt, "Are you ready for a restart?"

"I sure am," Kurt said.

"That's the attitude," Dr. McCarthy replied. "We have to get that heart back into condition, and it begins with restarting the dream."

FIVE

The Surgery

Sandy went out to the ICU waiting area. The two police officers that had escorted her to the hospital were still waiting. To Sandy, the officers looked so young. It reminded her of when Kurt first started on the force, which seemed so many years ago.

"How is he?" one of the officers asked.

"He's doing fine," Sandy replied confidently. "The doctor said he needed to rest, but they are going to do more tests to see how much damage was done to his heart."

"His heart?" the other officer responded.

Sandy continued to explain that Kurt had a heart attack and that his road to recovery looked promising. During the process of her explanation, the officers looked puzzled and confused. Sandy didn't make much of it; she brushed it off to their inexperience and immaturity. But in the back of her mind she wondered why they seemed so odd when she said Kurt had had a heart attack.

The officers reassured Sandy that someone from the precinct would be in touch with her. They said their goodbyes, and the men left.

They stood in the hallway waiting for the elevator. When the doors opened, Mary, Bryan and Lorrie exited as the officers entered the elevator.

Sandy saw the children and was glad they had arrived. She thanked Mary for handling things and bringing them to the hospital for her. She was in the process of explaining Kurt's condition to Mary and the children when Dr. McCarty walked into the waiting room. He wasn't wearing his white jacket, tie and dress slacks, but was in full scrubs.

"Sandy, can I speak to you for a moment," he asked.

"Sure," Sandy said.

The two of them stepped out into the hallway. Bryan, Lorrie and Mary watched as Dr. McCarty broke the news to Sandy.

Kurt was having complications. His condition had worsened since Sandy left. Only twenty minutes had gone by, and Dr. McCarty wanted to stabilize Kurt before the children could be permitted to see him.

Dr. McCarty walked off and Sandy returned to the waiting area. She explained the best she could to Bryan and Lorrie that their Dad was experiencing some minor setbacks, but not to worry. It was just going to take some time before they could go see their dad.

The children were getting restless and anxious. Forty-five minutes went by and still no word from anyone. Mary offered to take Bryan and Lorrie to the cafeteria and get them something to eat. Sandy felt it was a good idea, hoping it would stop them from worrying about Kurt.

The kids left with Mary; and Sandy was there alone. She looked at the table stand beside her. There lay a number of magazines, most of them out of date. She sorted through them, one by one. Time. . . People. . . Reader's Digest. Finally, she picked one . . . Better Homes and Gardens. One of the articles featured recipes. She loved to cook. She read each one and envisioned herself cooking them in her new kitchen, daydreaming which one Kurt would like best.

Lost in her own world of cooking Asparagus Egg Sandwiches, she suddenly noticed a pair of sneakers in her view. A young nurse, maybe 22 or 23 years old stood there staring at Sandy.

"Mrs. Dungy?" she asked in a high-pitched voice.

"Yes, that's me," Sandy said.

"Dr. McCarty will be down in a few minutes to speak with you," the nurse said directly with little or no emotion.

"Is everything all right?" Sandy asked. "It's been over an hour and my kids want to see their dad," she continued.

"Your husband has been moved from MICU to CICU . . . it's on the eleventh floor," the nurse replied.

"You've moved . . . why . . . and where am I. . ." Sandy nervously stammered her words, trying to put her thoughts together. She began to ponder, *where do I go now . . . why did I let the kids leave . . . how will I find them?*

"Just follow the hallway to the left and take the elevators to the eleventh floor. There is a waiting room to the right when you exit the elevator. Wait there and Dr. McCarty will come and speak with you," the nurse said.

"But my kids . . . my friend Mary . . . she took them to the cafeteria and . . ." Sandy spouted aloud as she stood up and began to pace the floor.

"You go ahead. I will inform the attendant at the nurses' station to alert your friend. Someone will assist them."

Sandy felt like she was losing her composure. She wanted to cry, but she held herself together. The nurse could tell she was overwhelmed.

"I promise, Mrs. Dungy . . . we will take care of it," the nurse said, trying to reassure Sandy that everything would be okay.

However, things were not okay. Unbeknown to Sandy, Kurt had suffered another heart attack, and several doctors and nurses were tending to him at that very moment.

Just then, Mary and the children exited the elevator and began to walk down the hallway. Sandy saw them coming and went out to greet them.

"Dad's been moved to another room. Let's take the elevator to the eleventh floor," Sandy said as she wrapped one arm around Lorrie and the other around Bryan. Mary took one look at Sandy and could tell something was definitely not right. She pretended not to notice, lest she frighten the kids unnecessarily. Sandy thanked the nurse, and the four of them walked toward the elevator.

Dr. McCarty entered the surgery room as his assistants began moving the cardiopulmonary bypass machine, a common apparatus used in open-heart surgeries, into position. It is a mechanical device that is a combination of a pump and an oxygenator which acts a substitute for the heart and lungs circulating blood flow during a surgery.

The room was 20' x 20'. Several nurses were busy organizing and laying the surgical instruments on dozens of movable stands scattered throughout the room. The physician's assistant was removing a vein from Kurt's leg for the bypass, as the anesthesiologist stood over Kurt's head monitoring his breathing and cardiac function on the echocardiogram device positioned directly over the top of Kurt.

The test revealed that Kurt had a clogged artery and needed surgery immediately. He was prepped, cut open and ready for surgery. The physician's assistant was making his final cuts to remove a vein from Kurt's leg. Only five more minutes and Dr. McCarty would begin his one-hour surgical procedure, but not before his normal routine.

Dr. McCarty nodded to the nurse. She proceeded with turning on the sound device by pressing the "on" button. The acoustics were not great, but the electric guitars blended as the drums rolled. Then the artists began performing as Dr. McCarty joined in singing aloud like a novice karaoke performer:

"I looked out this morning and the sun was gone.

Turned on some music to start my day;

I lost myself in a familiar song.

I closed my eyes and I slipped away. . ."

The nurses chuckled behind their face coverings as they watched Dr. McCarty play his "air" guitar to the sound of *More Than a Feeling* by Boston. It was something they were used to by now, but they still found it humorous to watch a professional heart surgeon mimic his favorite 80's rock-n-roll band as he mentally prepared and pumped up his adrenaline before surgery.

Dr. McCarty was ready and the surgery was underway. He inserted some sutures in the heart to prevent bleeding before injecting heparin. Dr. McCarty needed to make some stitches in order to properly connect the bypass. The vein was cleaned and prepped. Next, they installed the tubes for the heart/lung machine.

"Go on bypass!" Dr. McCarty shouted aloud.

The blood started pumping through the tube allowing Kurt's heart to deflate, allowing the movement to decrease and permitting Dr. McCarty to sew the vein successfully.

Without warning something went wrong!

"Blood pressure's dropping," a nurse declared.

"Clamp!" Dr. McCarty shouted.

A chest clamp was attached to spread Kurt's rib cage to enlarge the opening.

"Stop suction!" Dr. McCarty shouted.

"Heart rate 159," another nurse informed the surgical staff.

Kurt's heart went into fibrillation. Dr. McCarty watched as Kurt's heart rushed into unsynchronized contractions. His heart was pumping erratically and rapidly.

"We're losing him!" the assistant surgeon declared in a high-pitched voice.

Everything went crazy. Nurses were shouting as Dr. McCarty attempted to assess the problem. Kurt was having another attack, one that was undetected in their original synopsis. Everyone shuffled around, but it was too late. After several attempts, Kurt's heart could not be revived.

"Time of death . . . 11:07 AM."

SIX

The Dark Tunnel

Sheer solitude… was the atmosphere as Dr. McCarty stood silent at the sink as he washed his hands. Several nurses and physicians removed their gloves and gowns. Dr. McCarty turned and removed the paper towels from the dispenser, drying his forearms, looking down; he viewed his bloody gown resting lifeless in the hamper.

A drop of Kurt's blood was on his right booty. All he could think of was having to face Sandy. It was bad enough that he had to give her bad news, but the children . . . *they never got to talk to their dad,* he thought.

Dressed in his blue scrubs, Dr. McCarty exited the OR and proceeded to walk toward the CICU waiting room. Although he dreaded this part of the job, he had done it so many times before; he had his speech down to a science. The script was predictable, "I'm very sorry, we did everything we could . . . his heart just gave out."

As he entered the room, Bryan was playing a game on his phone. Lorrie was watching a morning show on the TV screen positioned high in the corner. Mary and Sandy were conversing.

Sandy turned to see Dr. McCarty walking in their direction. She saw a blank look. *Oh, no . . .* she thought to herself. Sandy stood as Dr. J came closer.

"He didn't make it. . . I'm sorry," he said.

The news was more than Sandy could take. She collapsed immediately to her knees. Mary attempted to grab her arm, but she missed. She hit the carpeted concrete floor like a brick.

"Mom," Bryan cried out, quickly dropping his phone in the empty seat beside him.

Lorrie turned and watched her mother sob in sorrow.

~

There must have been more than 80 police officers present at the grave site of every rank from the local precincts in which Kurt served faithfully for more than 15 years. Sandy, Lorrie and Bryan, dressed in all black, sat in their seats stone-faced as they listened to the sound of taps and a 21 gun salute that followed.

Hundreds of people, many whom Sandy never knew, came to the reception hosted at a local fire department hall where many of the town's people attended once a month auctions and bingo every Tuesday night.

Devastated and distraught, Sandy did her best to appear strong, but inside she was dying. Bryan had not said more than two words in three days and Lorrie stayed in her room avoiding visitors at their home. Sandy's mom spent hours trying to console Lorrie and her emotions, but to no avail.

Three months later, Bryan was suspended from school for fighting. The principal tried to show mercy, knowing that Bryan's father had recently passed, but when he questioned Bryan about his behavior, Bryan told the principal where to go . . . and it wasn't heaven. So, his hands were tied . . . three days suspension.

Things grew worse. Bryan was skipping school. Lorrie stopped attending band rehearsal. Creditors started calling. Once Sandy received Kurt's life insurance, she would be able to pay off most of the bills. Nevertheless, the sale of their previous home fell through after they signed on the new one. The realtor helped Kurt and Sandy get a bridge loan and delay the payments on their new home for three months, with the hope and promise that the old house would eventually sell — but it didn't.

Bryan continued to get into trouble. Eventually, he was expelled for excessive absenteeism, fighting, and out of school suspension. He was forced into anger management classes and counseling. Sandy had to enroll him in a detention school for troubled kids.

Lorrie turned bitter, bitter at her mom for showing so much attention to Bryan. Even though it was nothing more than Sandy reacting to her son's outburst, she was doing the best she could, and Lorrie's disapproval rating wasn't helping matters any.

After several months, Sandy was back in the office of her attorney who was handling the trust. Kurt had cashed in on most of his retirement and borrowed money against his living will to invest in a "dot com" company that tanked nine years earlier. Sandy was devastated with the news. There was no money for the kid's college fund, she was probably going to lose the house, and the attorney fees were astronomical.

Over the next few years, things deteriorated. Sandy had to sell the home and move into a 1200 square foot three-bedroom apartment. Instead of adjusting to a new school, Bryan gravitated to a negative group of friends that led him down the wrong path. He continued to rebel and was arrested several times. At age 17, he was placed in a boys' home about 45 miles west of Chicago. Sandy was only able to visit him twice a month, and their conversations caused her more frustrations as Bryan lashed out. The counselor informed Sandy that Bryan had a lot of resentment toward Kurt, and his pain was causing him to act out.

Lorrie spent all her time in her room on her computer surfing social media sites and chatting with virtual friends across the globe. Her way of dealing with matters was to confide in people who lived far away from her and her situation. Lorrie developed an online relationship with a boy in Louisville. His lack of maturity and responsibility was demonstrated when he convinced Lorrie she could come and live with him and his mom; after all, his mom was sympathetic and willing to drive to Chicago and get Lorrie.

Instead, Lorrie saved her lunch money and babysitting tips long enough until she could afford a bus ticket. Sandy came home that day from her job, where she waited on tables at a local diner in the suburbs, only to find that Lorrie was not home. She quickly started making phone calls, but Lorrie had disengaged herself from her friends at school, and no one knew where she was or where she would go.

By nine o'clock, Lorrie still had not shown up; she was not answering Sandy's texts and all calls went straight to voice mail. Sandy called Mike, Kurt's former partner and friend, to see if he could help. Mike agreed to investigate. Sandy would have called earlier, but she was not sure how long she needed to wait before filing a missing person's report. Mike reassured Sandy that she could file immediately, and that it's a misconception to what you see on television in reference to waiting 72 hours. But he still asked her several questions as to where she may have gone and why.

Immediately, Mike and his department were able to get information to local hospitals, bus stations, shelters and non-profit organizations that provide food and clothing to the homeless on the southwest side of Chicago.

It didn't take long. Only twenty minutes after posting information, the Greyhound bus station on North Broadway in Aurora called Mike's precinct to report a possible sighting of Lorrie. She had purchased a ticket for an 8:00 departure to Louisville, but her bus was late, apparently, it had mechanical problems in Detroit and was behind schedule.

Lorrie and a few passengers decided to go get a bite to eat. A Greyhound employee informed them that there were several restaurants three blocks down and across the Fox River. They walked down Broadway and crossed the New York St. Bridge. Halfway across, they heard the sounds of music coming from the Hollywood Casino. Some of the bus passengers opted to head down the stairs to the casino, but Lorrie and two other girls, Carrie and Jaclyn, continued over the bridge.

Carrie was 18, preppy, outgoing and a chatterbox. She was from Louisville and was in town to visit her cousin in south Chicago. Jaclyn was 19, with a gothic look . . . black nails, black hair, black clothes, and large holes in her earlobes. Her outward appearance was a mask to cover her insecurities, but she was a friendly and sweet-natured person.

She lived in Chicago and was on her way to Indianapolis to visit a college in hopes of attending that fall.

The three of them reached Lincoln Highway, also called River Street, and asked a cab driver that was parked on the side of the street where the closest restaurant was located.

"Two blocks down on the left . . . New China Hut," he said.

The streetlights shone brightly lighting up the upscale suburb of Aurora. The new brick buildings and shops lined up and down each side of the street demonstrated a curb appeal for an upper class area. The girls walked past a taco restaurant across the street, but passed it up and continued until they reached New China Hut. Lorrie and her two new friends wanted to eat quickly and get back to the bus station and not miss the awaited bus.

They ordered their food and sat down. Lorrie had not eaten at a Chinese restaurant before because of health reasons, so she needed some guidance with the menu.

"You gonna eat that?" Carrie asked Jaclyn as she pointed to her egg roll.

"No, I'm not into cabbage," Jaclyn replied.

"What is it?" Lorrie asked.

"You've never had an egg roll?" Carrie inquired.

"No," Lorrie answered.

"I think they're gross," Jaclyn said.

Carrie picked up the egg roll and offered it to Lorrie, "Try it. You'll like it," she said.

Lorrie hesitated and just stared at it.

"It ain't gonna bite you," Carrie insisted.

Lorrie accepted the offering and took a bite. She nodded her head as she chewed, insinuating that it tasted all right.

"Not bad," Lorrie commented.

"Told ya," Carrie replied.

~

Meanwhile, Mike Shell and his patrol partner, Thomas Gardner, arrived at the Greyhound bus station. The employee that gave the three girls the restaurant directions confirmed that Lorrie was one of several passengers waiting for an incoming bus and had gone down the street to get something to eat. After Mike gathered more information as to Lorrie's possible whereabouts, the two officers reentered the patrol car and called into dispatch.

Mike pulled out of the bus station to drive to the area he believed Lorrie might have gone. While en route, the cruiser was interrupted by an ambulance that sped by them on its way to a nearby hospital. Mike and Thomas saw a crowd outside the New China Hut. They parked the cruiser and investigated the situation.

When Mike and Thomas reached the restaurant doors, Charlie and Rob, two officers from the same precinct as Mike, were interviewing some girls standing in the lobby area.

"Mike . . . Thomas," Charlie said, greeting his follow officers.

"Whatcha got here?" Mike asked.

"10-33," Rob answered.

"We saw the ambulance . . . what happened?" Thomas asked.

"Allergic reaction," Rob said.

"To what?" Thomas inquired.

"Egg roll," Charlie answered.

"For real?" Thomas said with a slight chuckle in his voice.

Mike looked around at the crowd looking to see if he could locate Lorrie.

"Guys we're on an 805," Mike said.

"Who's missing?" Charlie asked.

"Lorrie Dungy, possible runaway . . . age 16 . . . brown hair . . . blue eyes . . . 5' 5"," Mike answered.

"Dungy? Rings a bell," Charlie replied.

"It should, it's Kurt Dungy's daughter," Mike responded.

"Sergeant Dungy, the guy who died a few years ago of a heart attack on a 211A?" Rob asked.

Mike showed a picture of Lorrie to Rob and Charlie.

"Is this the girl who went to the hospital?" Mike asked.

"Didn't get a good look . . . the EMT's arrived before us, and the girl had a rash all over her face," Charlie explained.

"But these two girls were eating with her when she collapsed," Rob said, pointing to Carrie and Jaclyn.

"Have you seen this girl?" Mike asked the girls.

"Hey, that's Lorrie," Carrie said.

Carrie and Jaclyn explained that they had just met Lorrie at the bus station. They were eating and after taking two bites of an egg roll, Lorrie immediately broke out in a rash and began to choke.

"I asked her if she was all right and all she said was 'peanuts,'" Jaclyn said.

Lorrie was allergic to peanuts, and most Chinese egg rolls are made from peanut flour. Lorrie was unaware that the Asian appetizer was as deadly as poison in her system. She counted on her mom to tell her what foods she could eat.

Mike called Sandy to inform her they had located Lorrie. Sandy was relieved they had found her, but worried about her condition.

Mike, Thomas and Sandy got to the hospital around the same time. They stood in the ER waiting area as Mike explained how they had located Lorrie.

A tall, bald-headed doctor dressed in blue scrubs walked into the waiting room. Mike nodded as if to announce his arrival. Sandy turned around and, when she did, she thought she saw a ghost. It was Kurt's surgeon, Dr. McCarty.

"I'm sorry, we did everything we could, but Lorrie didn't make it."

Sandy didn't even have time to process the information before collapsing onto the floor. She pounded her fists on the floor screaming at the top of her lungs, "No… No…. not again!"

Charlie just stood there, not knowing what to say.

Mike walked away in shock. *Oh my gosh… this can't be happening,* he thought. . . *Sandy will never bounce back from this. She lost everything since Kurt's. . .*

"Is he back?"

Mike turned around and looked at the doctor, "What did you say?"

"He's back!" Dr. McCarty exclaimed.

"What the hell are you talking about?" Mike demanded.

"Give me vitals," the doctor called.

Tears streaming down her face, Sandy lifted her head and said, "Who's back?"

"Kurt's back," he declared.

~

Dr. McCarty looked up at the clock; it read, 11:07. "He's back! Vitals?" he said.

The nurses responded:

"Heart rate 140."

"120 over 77."

"Oxygen 97."

"Oh, my God," Dr. McCarty said as he took a deep breath.

"You've never lost anyone when you've played 'More Than a Feeling,'" the physician's assistant remarked to Dr. McCarty.

"Well, it's official then," the doctor said. "From now on, Boston is my lucky band and we will dedicate it to Kurt Dungy, the cop that almost got away."

SEVEN

About the Heart

Sheer enthusiasm... was the atmosphere as Dr. McCarty stood smiling at the sink as he washed his hands. Several nurses and physicians were laughing aloud as they removed their gloves and gowns. Dr. McCarty turned and removed the paper towels from the dispenser, drying his forearms; looking down, he viewed his bloody gown resting lifeless in the hamper. It made him appreciate that Kurt had been given a second chance — something not afforded to everyone. This was his big break.

It had been nearly five hours since Dr. McCarty had talked to Sandy. He looked forward to sharing the good news.

"He's doing fine," Dr. McCarty said.

He took about ten minutes to explain the surgery, Kurt's condition, and when they could see him. By now Sandy's parents were present, along with Mike Shell and a few other friends who were in the business with Kurt and Sandy. They had arrived to the hospital and were in the ER waiting area — showing their support and comfort.

Dr. McCarty walked away, and Sandy gave a summary of what he shared with her about Kurt's surgery and his progress. Because Bryan and Lorrie were standing along with everyone else, Sandy decided it best not to mention that Kurt died in surgery and was gone for 1 minute and 19 seconds.

It wasn't long enough to cause any real threat to Kurt's brain, but 1 minute and 19 seconds seemed like years for Kurt. His out-of-body experience was an incident that would shape Kurt's outcome, sort of like an epiphany — if you would. At first, he could see the doctors and nurses working on his body in the ER and then, like watching a movie screen, Kurt observed what life would be like without him. The sheer pain in Bryan and Lorrie, how his decisions crushed Sandy devastated Kurt. It was so real to him. He would never forget it.

Sandy was able to see Kurt, but he had a trach tube which prevented him from talking. Bryan and Lorrie visited for about five minutes and they left that evening anxious to return the next day.

Sandy and the children returned the next morning arriving around 9 o'clock. The nurses had removed the tracheotomy tube, which allowed Kurt to talk, but his throat was still sore. Sandy entered his room around 9:20. The head nurse, Holly, informed Sandy that if Kurt did well, he would be moved from CICU to MICU within a day or two. That was a positive sign.

Sandy walked in alone. Bryan and Lorrie were in the CICU waiting area with Sandy's parents. She came close the bed and paused. Kurt was resting and she didn't want to wake him. The nurses worked on his machines, IV's, and had removed the trach earlier that morning, some-time around 6:30. Her emotions were about to get the best of her, when Kurt adjusted his head on the pillow and opened his eyes long enough to see her standing next to him. He smiled.

His lips were dry, his face unshaved and patches of a white beard appeared on his chin. Sandy reached down, grasped Kurt's hand, and then she gently squeezed it to reinforce her love and support. Their eyes connected. Sandy noticed a tear form in the corner of his eye and gravity pulled it down his cheek. It flowed rapidly like a stream and landed on his pillow. Sandy reached up with her hand, wiped the tear streak from his face and said, "It's going to be all right."

"I'm so sorry. . ." Kurt said in a soft weak tone.

"Shh, you don't need to be sorry," Sandy replied.

"There are so many things I'll do different once I get out of here," Kurt reassured.

"We'll just take it a day at a time, baby," Sandy said.

Kurt's eyes suddenly enlarged and his heart rate increased rapidly, causing his monitor to start beeping.

"Honey, are you alright? Do you need me to get a nurse?" Sandy asked with deep concern.

Kurt started to cry even more, tears streaming down both sides of his face.

"What is it honey?" Sandy asked.

Kurt tried to talk, but his throat was dry and his emotions choked him even more. Sandy saw a styrofoam cup on a stand near his bed. It was chipped ice with a small straw and a minute spoon on the other end. She scooped up a small portion of ice and placed it in Kurt's mouth.

Kurt closed his eyes as the ice melted in his mouth and swallowed. He tried to talk again but his voice was too soft for her to hear, so Sandy bent over the railing of the bed to get closer.

"Is Lorrie allergic to peanuts?" Kurt asked.

Still leaning over the rail, Sandy leaned up to look into Kurt's eyes. "No," Sandy said.

Kurt choked and let out a gasp of relief, "Thank God." When he did, his lips quivered and with a sense of joy, he began to cry.

"What's this about?" Sandy inquired.

Kurt proceeded to explain to Sandy what happened to him while he was in surgery. He told how he could see the doctors and nurses working on him as he floated above. Then he watched the events of the future, a future without him, unfold before him. He told how Bryan rebelled and ended up in a boy's home for troubled teens. Then, how Lorrie reclused into seclusion and ran away. How Sandy struggled to pay the bills, later she lost the house and finally, how she fell apart when Lorrie died.

"It was just a dream," Sandy replied.

"No, I wasn't asleep . . . I was dead, for 1 minute and 19 seconds," Kurt said affirmatively.

"But it wasn't real," Sandy remarked.

"It was real to me, and I am not going to allow our family to suffer anymore," Kurt said.

The next day, Monday, Kurt was doing much better. Bryan and Lorrie went to school and were going to come to the hospital later that day. Sandy arrived again shortly after 9:00 AM.

When she entered his room, Kurt was sitting up, alert, and looking much better despite the fact he had not shaved in three days. Flowers were arriving nearly every fifteen minutes and the shelf against the window was full of arrangements.

They sat and talked for over an hour before Dr. McCarty made his rounds and landed in Kurt's room.

"Good morning," Dr. McCarty said with a smile. He was always so cheerful and positive. "You're looking much better today."

"I feel much better . . . a little sore," Kurt said as he placed his hand on his chest, ever so gently.

"Yeah, those ribs will be sore for a few days or more, but before you know it, you'll feel much better," the doctor replied.

"I'm looking forward to that," Kurt said.

Dr. McCarty pulled a stool over to the bed and sat down. Sandy was sitting on the other side of Kurt's bed. "I think it's important we have a chat about why you had an MLM heart attack."

"Okay," Kurt said.

"These were your vital signs," Dr. McCarty pointed to a chart he had on a clipboard. "These signs tell us a lot about what was going on before, and why you are here today.

"Simply put, Kurt, vital signs are the indicators, the gauges of your heart. They tell us what you're doing and not doing. Your heart pumps blood to the rest of your body. The blood carries oxygen — energy — that is necessary for survival. The oxygen is the relationship that gives life, and it circulates back to your heart. You see, Kurt, the heart is the science of the business. I think you have fallen into the trap so many others have — focusing on the wrong things. In this business, it's 10% mechanics and 90% relationships.

"Here is my diagnosis. When you first get involved in MLM you have a natural excitement that carries you through when it comes to talking to your first few dozen presentations. Your friends get involved with you because they trust you, and they join you because they can see how excited you are.

"But, when the original excitement has worn off, you need something else to see you through. The thing that sees you through are the people that you meet. When you go to an MLM meeting or a training session, you'll find yourself surrounded by bright, cheerful, positive people . . . people who have dreams and are actively doing something about them. As much as MLM has its detractors, and it would be stupid to suggest that it doesn't, the people who knock it don't attend events. They don't get to be around the positive influences . . . the ones who keep us motivated and maintain our beliefs when it would be so easy to quit. They don't get to make the friends that are there to help when we need it.

"The heart of the MLM business is relationships. If you cut yourself off from relationships, a ripple effect begins. You must touch people first before you can ever change their lives. When I say, 'touch,' I mean emotionally, and in the heart. They must feel your sincerity. They must know you are there to help them, not sell them something. People know when we are takers and not givers. They don't want hype. They want your passion. Emotion is what puts the heart, and the person, in motion to move towards success.

"A healthy heart produces success. This is the secret to the heart, to get people moving toward you, then with you, and then for you. The heart is the success magnet that draws people to you, and not away. Kurt, people are magnetized to a strong emotion of the heart, and that is what touches the person, and their heart.

"A healthy heart produces possibilities, dreams and hope. Hope for a better life. Hope for a better lifestyle. Hope for a better future. But, if you don't learn how to serve others, others will not serve you. Once that happens, relationships fall apart, dreams fall apart and hope escapes the heart.

"If you lose the hope in the heart, you stop taking care of yourself. Your heart weakens, blockage builds up, and eventually you have an MLM heart attack. Your obstacles get bigger than your dreams. Before you know it, the people who say "no" clog your heart, and it paralyzes you. You give up. And over time, your heart quits.

"My goal is twofold. To get you strong enough to start therapy and refer you to a good therapist who can help you restart your heart.

"My job is to repair the damage, but a therapist's job is to get you stronger and give you techniques that will not only prevent another MLM heart attack, but give you the ability to help others avoid what you're going through right now.

"A therapist will teach you how to stay in a positive zone. She's going to tell you that you should be reading and listening to books and CDs to stay active and healthy and how proper exercise will rebuild your heart. That means practice every day to get busy doing the business, and then to eat a balanced diet. That means stay away from negativity. Keep lots of positivity in your life.

"You will learn the importance of the heart. First, you touch the heart, then change. If you don't touch the emotions somewhere along the lines, by truly caring about the person and cultivating healthy relationships, not just a paycheck, they probably will not embrace your concept.

"People have dreams and desires, and your job, Kurt, as an MLM leader is to help them accomplish their dreams with your leadership and business plan. They want to know you are coming from the heart — a healthy heart — and want to touch their hearts with hope and a real chance to make their dreams come true by leading them there.

"It's all about the heart."

EIGHT

Recovery

Three days had passed since Kurt was brought into the hospital. His chest was still a bit sore, but his mobility and appetite were much better. The first two days, Kurt felt like he'd been hit by a truck and then run over by a bulldozer. He still had wires and tubes coming in and out of his body. Every morning, the nurses would wake Kurt up and make him get out of bed. First, he just sat on the edge of the bed. Next, he was standing and taking a few steps to a chair in the room. The nurses gave Kurt instructions on how to move about, minimizing the pain, and how to protect the surgical wound.

Kurt was thankful for the pain medicine. The hospital had several pamphlets with instructions to make life change decisions that would encourage recovery. After all, open-heart bypass surgery is not a cure for heart disease. A patient who does not follow the doctor's instructions to make the right changes may find that their coronary artery disease has returned and is blocking the new grafts.

Dr. McCarty told Kurt that he would be coming by on the third day to give him some information and instructions before he would release him to go home.

Home, sweet home, was on Kurt's mind. He could not wait to get back to his family. The epiphany from his out-of-body experience was still heavy on Kurt's mind. He could not help but think how fortunate he was for a second chance.

It was Kurt's "Aha" moment . . . a wakeup call to reality. This was his time. He spent time lying in his hospital bed reflecting, contemplating and summarizing his past, his present and his future. Kurt knew he had to make significant life-altering changes to his lifestyle if he was to live life to its fullest. There was no way he could survive if he went back to life as it was. It was time for a change and he was ready.

He sat in his chair thinking about what type of things he would need to change when Sandy came back from the cafeteria. Sandy and Kurt discussed some of the changes they wanted to make when Dr. McCarty entered the room.

"Hello, Kurt . . . Sandy," Dr. McCarty greeted them. "How are you doing today?" he asked Kurt.

"Ready to go home," Kurt answered.

"I'm sure you are," Dr. McCarty replied. "But first, I want to follow up on our previous conversation as to what you need to do to restart the heart.

"Kurt, looking over your chart, I've learned that you were in network marketing before, and now that you've had an MLM heart attack, I think the first step is to rejoin your group and commit yourself to a team again. The process of restarting your heart begins with you revisiting the dream. The first thing you have to find out is, why do you want to do it?"

"Do the business?" Kurt asked.

"Yes," Dr. McCarty answered.

"I'm sick of my job. I need a new job. Secondly, I want to spend more time with my kids."

"And how's that been working out for you?" Dr. J said.

"Nothing's changed. I never get to see them. I hate my job."

"When you first joined your business, you felt excitement. What did you believe was possible to achieve?"

Kurt paused for a second, "I could really see that I could be different — that I could quit my job."

"Would you like that, Kurt?"

"Of course."

"And how much money would it take from doing this business, so you would be able to quit your job?"

"Well," Kurt perked up, "I'm making $3,000 a month now, so if I was making at least that much, I could quit my job."

"So if I could show you, and the therapist could help you develop an income of, say $5,000, and help you retire from your job, would that excite you?"

"Oh, yeah," Kurt answered with a smile. Sandy grinned and looked at Kurt. It was as if the dream was beginning to rekindle inside of them.

"The first step, Kurt and Sandy, is revisiting the dream. When you get home, I want you to take a pen and a notebook that will become your "restart the heart" journal and write out your dream. Once you've done that, then your therapist will help you in step two.

"Step two is clarifying your goals. You will need a solid plan and specific targets to aim toward. These targets are the progression of you reaching your grand goal of making $3-5,000 a month so you can quit your job. But it begins with a realistic strategy and a short-term target. Once you achieve that, then you go on to the next target and so on.

"But it's important for you, as the patient, to see the necessity of a therapist. Think of it like this; as an MLM heart attack patient, you are the apprentice, or a novice. As an apprentice, you are bound by indenture to serve another for a prescribed period with a view of learning an art or a trade.

"In other words, you need to realize this as a redo, a restart, or starting from the beginning. You see, Kurt, when a prospect joins the business, he becomes the apprentice. I love the term apprentice because it describes perfectly the mental state of the person who joins the business, and it sets the right mindset for the sponsor. Think about when a student gets his certificate or degree as an automobile mechanic, or an engineer, or a doctor, or a lawyer. The student is simultaneously excited and scared. Excited because the classroom education is done and now he can start paying off those student loans and scared because now he is on his own. Now think about those first couple of months as an apprentice. The apprentice is monitored closely, given enough room to work and to move forward, but only under the watchful eye of a journeyman who has the 10,000 hours. One who has been around the block and got the t-shirt.

"As an apprentice, you need a therapist, or a mentor. In a perfect world, a 'Responsible Sponsor' would have introduced you into the business. Sadly, that is seldom the case. You need a person who cares about you and is willing to pour into you so you can succeed and get your heart back in the condition it needs to be."

"But I'm not ready for physical therapy yet, am I?" Kurt asked.

"Well, yes and no," Dr. McCarty replied. "Full-blown therapy, no, but sometimes the mental therapy prepares you for the physical therapy. You can start out with exercises that will equip you for what is next. You're not going to get better overnight. It takes time.

"I want you to start reading some books and listening to some CDs — they'll stretch you and assist you in your recovery.

"Take for instance," Dr. McCarty picked up a book called *The Most Important Minute* off the portable stand and showed it to Kurt and Sandy as he began to explain, "how you think and view things. Your view will either cloud or enhance your vision. The most important attitude for financial success is long-term thinking. Successful people think a long way into the future and they adjust their daily behaviors to ensure they achieve their long-term goals.

"Poor people's thinking is 'Life happens to me.' If you wish to be successful, it is important that you believe you are the person behind the wheel of your life. You create every single second of your life, especially your financial life.

"Kurt, let me ask you this, what do most people do when they need money?"

"Go in debt?" Kurt answered.

"Exactly. Some borrow and get deeper in debt. Others tighten their belts and adjust their needs to their meager income. Instead of challenging themselves and their world to fulfill their dreams, most people limit their dreams to their perceptions of the world's limitations. They have a passive, wait-and-see attitude and say something like, 'If this happens to me, it will be a miracle.' And with that kind of attitude, it doesn't happen."

Kurt was glued to every word Dr. McCarty was saying. It was making more sense, maybe because Kurt was out of options, but it was more than just that . . . he really wanted to change the way things were. He knew he had failed miserably and he wanted to make it up to Sandy, Bryan and Lorrie.

"Here's another one," Dr. McCarty said as he handed Kurt a book. "I think you'll like this one," he said with a grin on his face.

Kurt glanced at the front cover, read the title, gave the doctor a puzzled look and said, "Beach Money . . . what's that about?"

"If you really want to quit your job, you need this book," Dr. McCarty responded. "This guy spent 9 years trying to make it in the business. He had some setbacks, but he didn't stop trying."

Dr. McCarty had a plastic bag with some CDs. He handed it to Sandy and encouraged them to listen to them and return them whenever they were done. He continued to explain to Kurt the importance of creating a new plan to get healthy and things he could do to develop new habits.

After about twenty minutes, Dr. McCarty told Kurt that if nothing changed in his conditions, he could be released sometime the next day.

"But before you go," Dr. McCarty said as he stood up and took two steps toward the door, "I will be introducing you to your therapist, Dr. Kay Donaldson. I'll make the arrangements."

"Okay," Kurt said.

Great, just what I need. . . Kurt thought as the doctor left.

He wasn't sure if he was more anxious about physical therapy or that his therapist was a woman. Kurt had a big ego and all his supervisors were men.

NINE

Relapse

The next morning, Sandy arrived earlier than usual.

Fortunately for her, but not in Kurt's opinion, Sandy's mother agreed to stay at their house for an undermined amount of time to help with the kids and assist Sandy around the house. So Nana, as Bryan and Lorrie called her, was going to take them to school that morning, which gave Sandy the ability to get to the hospital around 6:30 AM.

It was Kurt's release day and he was scheduled to get a shower and shave, but he wasn't quite ready to lift his arms that high or long to shampoo his head or shave his burly bearded face. Sandy willingly agreed; she was the best candidate to assist Kurt with these personal hygiene issues, and not a nurse.

It was about ten minutes to eight when Dr. McCarty arrived with Dr. Kay Donaldson, Kurt's therapist. Dr. Kay introduced herself to Kurt and Sandy, and then proceeded to explain the process of rehabilitation. At first Kurt was going to spend a few days regaining his strength and mobility. Simple things like walking and getting up out of a chair unassisted were his baby steps.

By week two, Kurt was to visit Dr. Kay at her office for a checkup. If all went well, Kurt was to come to the Physical Therapy Center, just a few blocks from the hospital, where he would begin a series of three days a week in physical therapy. In addition, a treadmill would be provided in his home for additional exercises.

By 11:00, Kurt signed his release papers. A male nurse entered the room with a wheel chair to escort Kurt to the outpatient curb.

"Mr. Dungy, you ready to ride out of here?" he said.

"More than ready," Kurt replied.

Sandy and Kurt talked about how the kids were handling his hospital stay. Sandy expressed how sad they were, but were looking forward to spending some quality time together with their dad.

Bryan and Lorrie got home from school around 3:30. Kurt was taking a nap in his favorite La-Z-boy chair in the den. Bryan walked in first and then Lorrie. The television was on, but Kurt was fast asleep.

Lorrie took the remote that was still clinched in Kurt's hand and turned off the TV. Kurt had fallen asleep watching his favorite channel, ESPN. When she did, Kurt woke up.

It startled Kurt, and he didn't have his bearings when he came to.

"I'm alright," he said as he stumbled in his chair.

"Dad, it's cool," Bryan said. He recognized that Kurt was awake and was unsure where he was. After all, waking up in the hospital all those days and now being at home was a bit different.

"Hey, guys," Kurt said to Bryan and Lorrie, "good to see you two."

Lorrie bent down to hug her dad.

"Carefully, his chest is still sore," Sandy said.

Kurt pulled his t-shirt up and exposed a portion of his scar.

"Dad!" Lorrie screeched, "that's gross!"

Bryan laughed, "You wimp."

Lorrie shoved Bryan and said, "Jerk!"

"Alright. . . Alright," Sandy said as she verbally broke up the sibling rivalry. "You two break it up; your dad needs some peace and quiet not a war," she remarked.

"Good to have you home, Dad," Bryan said.

"Good to be home," Kurt replied.

That evening after dinner, Kurt and Sandy sat in the den watching television and talking about the things that Dr. Kay shared relative to his physical therapy. Kurt wasn't resistant, but he wasn't looking forward to it.

The next morning, a Friday, the kids went off to school as Kurt sat at the kitchen table eating breakfast.

"Poached eggs?" Kurt said to Sandy as she put his plate on the table in front of him.

"It's on the list," Sandy replied in reference to the diet plan on Kurt's pamphlet she received from Dr. McCarty as "acceptable" food.

"You gotta be kidding me," Kurt responded as he stared at his plate. "You're killing me," he continued.

Kurt reached for the salt.

"Uh-uh," Sandy reacted, "no salt."

Kurt knew she was right, but he gave Sandy a definite look of disgust.

After breakfast Kurt took a short, twenty-minute nap. Sandy was busy doing laundry, and Kurt began to ponder his situation. He had only been home one day and already he was getting restless. Sitting around the house doing nothing wasn't what Kurt was used to. He could never sit still. All of a sudden, it hit him.

He couldn't go back to work any time soon. He was dependent upon Sandy for everything. Bryan's soccer game was on Saturday and he was not going to be able to go. He thought about his job on the police force, and it just frustrated him even more. He hated his job and all he thought about was going back to work after his recovery. And that didn't make him feel any better.

The next morning, Sandy and her mom took the kids to Bryan's soccer game. Kurt convinced Sandy to go, saying he would be all right. After all, it was only going to be two hours. He could handle it.

But twenty minutes later, Kurt was getting fidgety. He tried listening to one of the CDs Dr. McCarty gave him, but he drifted off, thinking about how long he would be laid up. What was he going to do about his financial future? How long was it going to take to get out of this mess? The mental anguish started to take its toll and Kurt was struggling with his emotions.

By that evening Kurt was acting out . . . being short with Sandy and having to apologize for his outburst. Sandy did all she could do, but Kurt was not accepting her sympathy and affection for his condition.

The next day, Sunday, Kurt sat in his chair watching the Cubs. When Sandy asked him if he had read any of the books or listened to any CDs, Kurt told her that he was going to start tomorrow.

Monday Kurt started to feel depressed. He tried to read a book, but after three pages he quickly forgot what he had read, so he put it down.

The next day Sandy took Kurt to Dr. Kay's office for his follow up visit. When asked how he was doing, Kurt said, "Just fine."

Sandy wanted to speak up and rebut Kurt's response, but she didn't want Kurt to feel frustrated, so she didn't say anything.

Two days later Kurt's depression escalated. He was struggling to walk to the bathroom. All he wanted to do was sit in his favorite chair and watch sports. Sandy tried to convince him he would feel better once he started physical therapy; Kurt was scheduled to begin the following Monday, and the thought of it raised Kurt's blood pressure.

Anxiety was settling in. Kurt would break out in a sweat for no reason. He continued to ask for more pain medication, but he had already reached his limit, and Sandy wasn't going to budge. That frustrated Kurt even more, and he tried to manipulate Sandy's emotions by saying she didn't care if he was in pain or not.

"That's not true," Sandy replied, "I do care, but too much medication is not going to help you. You need to get up out of that chair and get some exercise. Remember what Dr. McCarty said about building new plans and developing new habits?"

"Oh, so you're taking his side now?" Kurt snapped back.

"I'm not taking anyone's side but your's, Kurt, and I want you to get better. Taking more pain killers is not going to make it better," Sandy replied. "Besides, Dr. Kay said that you would have to press through the pain to get healthy."

Kurt leaned forward in his chair to continue his argument with Sandy when he started choking and coughing. Each cough felt like a punch in his chest. She tried to get him to take a drink, but Kurt couldn't stop coughing.

Kurt continued coughing and his face became deep red, almost a purple tone, when he fell out of his chair to the floor.

"I can't breathe! I can't breathe!" Kurt shouted in between coughs. "Call an ambulance! I'm having another heart attack!"

~

Kurt lay on the bed in the ER as the nurses and EMT discussed his vitals. Sandy was upset because her mother had just gone back home the day before, and now she was frantically trying to figure out who was going to be there when the kids got home from school.

An hour went by before Dr. McCarty came into the ER. The large room had approximately twenty individual stations, each separated by hanging curtains and equipped with all the medical equipment needed to tend to individual patients. The noise and commotion was a continuous reminder to his anxiety, and it aggravated Kurt to listen to the clamor.

Dr. McCarty entered the cubical where Kurt lay.

"What's going on?" the doctor asked.

"You tell me, you're the doctor," Kurt replied.

"Well, according to your vitals, everything looks normal, but we will run some tests just to be sure," Dr. McCarty said. "Let me ask you," he continued, "have you been reading the books or listening to the CDs I gave you?"

"I've tried . . . I just can't concentrate on that right now. I just want to get better so I can get back to work," Kurt responded.

"I see," the doctor said, "well, we'll run some tests and see what's going on. Then we'll decide what's next."

Dr. McCarty left the room. About forty-five minutes later, the nurses came in to take Kurt for his EKG. Meanwhile, Dr. McCarty caught up with Sandy in the ER waiting area to chat.

"Sandy, how's Kurt been acting the past ten days?" he asked.

"Real moody. He just wants to sit in his favorite chair and watch sports. He's not doing any exercises, and all he wants is his meds. I try to encourage him, but the more I do, the more he gets frustrated with me," Sandy said. Frustrated over the situation, she started to cry.

"Sandy, it's okay. Some patients have setbacks."

"Setbacks?" Sandy replied.

"Yes. . . Denial. . . Depression. . . Mood swings."

"Is that typical?" she asked.

"Well, when a person has an MLM heart attack, if they don't follow the plan, they will have a setback. The diet and exercise regimen is necessary. A proper diet provides the essential ingredients to develop a strong and healthy heart. There are foods that clog and foods that cleanse. There are habits that destroy our success and habits that build success.

"Kurt has to choose to change his mental atmosphere and environment. I call it a check up, from the neck up . . . stink'in think'in will paralyze your progress. It begins with a positive attitude and a strong desire to win. He needs to avoid stress by eliminating negative influences, negative people, negative ideas and sticking to the strategies we prescribe."

Dr. McCarty joined Kurt and Sandy in the ER. "The tests are negative," he said. "Kurt, you didn't have an MLM heart attack, it was a panic attack. You need to take the prescribed medicine for recovery and not choose to watch TV instead." It was time for a change in lifestyle and a wakeup call.

"Kurt," Dr. McCarty said, "if you don't do what you need to do to get better, then you're going to die!"

TEN

Therapy

Those words hit a chord. As soon as Kurt heard Dr. McCarty say, "Then you're going to die," his mind raced back to his out-of-body experience.

What am I doing? Kurt thought to himself as he lay on the bed in the ER. His mind raced to the epiphany, and he rehearsed the scenes in his mind . . . dying in surgery, Bryan getting in trouble with the law, Sandy losing the house, and his little princess, Lorrie, dying from peanut poisoning.

"Kurt? Kurt?" Sandy called, "Kurt, wake up. KURT!"

Kurt came out of his daze. He looked straight up and there stood Sandy.

"Where's Dr. McCarty?" Kurt asked.

"He left about two minutes ago," she answered, "are you all right?" Sandy inquired.

"I think so."

"Dr. McCarty said we could go now, you ready?"

Kurt didn't respond like she expected.

"Absolutely!"

Kurt returned home that day with a new outlook. He listened to some motivational CDs, four times in one a day.

Day 2: Kurt read *Beach Money* and *The Most Important Minute*.

Day 3: Kurt agreed to join a support group for MLM heart attack survivors.

Day 4: Kurt called Dr. McCarty and asked for more books.

Day 5: Kurt went to physical therapy.

Day 6: Kurt listened to 6 CDs.

Day 7: After therapy was done, Dr. Kay gave Kurt a book, *From Here to Having it All*. "I believe you're ready for this now, Kurt; I want you to read it and tell me what you think," Dr. Kay said.

Kurt took it. This was a milestone for him . . . not the reading a book part, but taking advice from a woman. Kurt had issues with submitting to a woman in leadership. He wasn't biased per se, just not accustomed to it. Kurt loved Sandy and respected women's rights, as long as he wasn't taking orders from one.

Maybe it was because most of the CDs he listened to were women who became multi-millionaires.

Riding home from therapy that day, they listened to one of the CDs from Kurt's collection. Sandy had grabbed one and brought it with her so she could listen, too.

"If you want to make it work in this business, you need to do more than put your foot in the water and give this a try. . . You have to believe in yourself first; otherwise, when people say "no," you will be devastated, take it personal and give up. You don't try . . . you decide!"

That evening, Kurt started reading the book Dr. Kay gave him earlier that day, *From Here to Having it All*. The author started out by giving his biography, and Kurt could relate to his story. It was about a former homicide detective in Toronto who did not grow up with a silver spoon in his mouth. Like most, the author's parents were not wealthy and this created a burning desire to be wealthy. His father worked a blue-collar job, as did Kurt's, and could not always afford the luxuries of life for his family. The book shared how the writer saw a need early in his career to change his personality. This hit home with Kurt, because the only thing holding him back from success was himself.

Kurt continued to read and learn about the writer's quest to improve his attitude and character. He needed to study people who possessed impeccable characteristics of integrity, influence and success. His research led the author to write about seven influential people: Mahatma Gandhi, Mother Teresa, Bill Gates, Warren Buffett, Steve Jobs, John F. Kennedy and Pierre Trudeau.

Kurt was on his third notebook. He had been compiling his own journal from the CDs he'd listened to and the books he had read. He opened to a blank page and penned the ten characteristics for highly successful people based upon the book he was reading that night:

1. Have a mentor — be a mentor
2. Be the best at your core task
3. Be an excellent communicator
4. Have a *why* that makes you cry
5. Be supremely confident
6. Be detail-oriented and learn to multi-task
7. Have a strong gravitational pull
8. Serve others; inspire trust and loyalty
9. Live in the present moment
10. Be action driven

~

Six weeks had gone by and Kurt was regaining his strength every day. At first, he went to physical therapy three times a week. Then it was two times a week, and now he was in his last week of therapy. Kurt was finally able to bench press for the first time. He had spent many days on a treadmill and a bicycle.

The group therapy was also helping. Kurt had invited so many friends to the meetings they had to move to a hotel. Kurt was so outspoken about how his MLM heart attack nearly destroyed his life and he had been given a second chance. His positive attitude was contagious, and those who knew the "old" Kurt Dungy didn't recognize the "new" Kurt Dungy.

Kurt had not only recovered from his MLM heart attack, he was showing others how to prevent one in their life.

Six months later Kurt went back to see Dr. Kay. She was proud of his progress. Kurt didn't have to return to physical therapy, but he stayed in contact with Dr. Kay. In fact, she was a regular speaker at his meetings.

The MLM heart association that Kurt started in his house was now averaging over 700 persons in a hotel. He was also conducting seminars, teaching and giving motivational speeches via Skype and Google+ to 147 MLM Healthy Heart Association groups across seventeen different states and webinars in Puerto Rico, Aruba, Costa Rica, London, and Canada.

The response was amazing. All Kurt did was share his story about his out-of-body experience when he died on the operating table during his open-heart bypass surgery.

Each day, Kurt used the exercise equipment at his house to get back into shape. Not only was his health improving, but also his MLM HHA was expanding beyond his wildest imagination. However, his biggest challenge was forthcoming. Next Monday, Kurt was scheduled to return to active duty. Sure, it's a desk job, answering phones, filing reports, going through case files and updating data on a computer . . . but going back to the police precinct was going to be a big adjustment for Kurt. His quest to help others build a strong heart had grown and took all his time. Now Kurt had to juggle his schedule, something he had not been faced with for a while.

Kurt had not been back to work more than three days, and already he was the brunt of many jokes and name calling in the locker room: "Get Richy," "The Million Dollar Man," and "Ponzi Cop." But it didn't affect Kurt one bit. It shocked quite a few officers as well. Back in the day, a name-calling session would have sent Kurt over the edge, and he'd probably take a swing or two. Not now — Kurt was confident in himself and his business. What others thought of him didn't matter. He had his eyes on his dream and nothing was going to stop him. The more they teased and made fun of him, the more it motivated Kurt to succeed so he could leave his job. Kurt determined in his heart that he was going to see it through to the end.

As crazy as it sounds, Kurt had the date "04/08/12" and the letters "REZ" in all caps tattooed on his right bicep. That was the day Kurt had open-heart bypass surgery and his out-of-body experience. In addition, it was Easter, so the letters REZ were an abbreviation for Resurrection Sunday, a religious holiday for Christians who celebrated the resurrection of Jesus Christ. It was a reminder of his second chance in life. Every time he looked at his tattoo in the mirror, or when someone asked about it, it would reinforce his epiphany episode and reemphasize his successful future. Kurt's success was based upon the system he learned from Dr. McCarty and strategies from Dr. Kay.

It was Dr. Kay who showed Kurt how to restart his heart. He learned to believe in himself, in his company, in his compensation plan and to believe in others. From then on, all Kurt needed to do was show how to cultivate people skills. Kurt duplicated what he learned and showed others how to do it too. The rest followed like dominoes or a ripple effect in a body of water.

First, he learned how to revisit the dream. The books and CDs created a mindset that helped him overcome his obstacles. Kurt realized his attitude determined his altitude. Instead of hounding those who were in his business, he cultivated relationships, looked for ways to help others, and discovered that 90% of the networking business was relationships and 10% mechanics. Kurt's character changed, and he wanted to become the change — no excuses, just results. He learned that becoming a great leader meant he had to manage people more than he had to manage products. He fell in love with his company and the people who worked in it. He realized he needed others. He was no longer a "lone ranger." The more he helped others reach their dream, the more Kurt's dream was beginning to take form. He learned to submit to Dr. Kay's advice. She knew more about building a healthy heart than anyone in Kurt's life.

Second, Kurt made a plan. He set goals for each month. It started with $500, then $1000 and by the sixth month, he was making $2000 per month.

Third, he made his list of names, potential prospects. Kurt started making presentations. Each month he increased, and by week seven he was up to 16 presentations per week. Dr. Kay taught him a script, and he did not deviate from it. He was booking more and more meetings until eventually, he was meeting in a hotel.

Fourth, Kurt learned how to "defrost" people. When people begin to object to the presentation, they freeze up. They get scared. Something the speaker said causes them to freeze and not want to move forward. Kurt became a master "defreezer." He eliminated confusion and helped people focus on the dream and not the obstacles.

Fifth, creating short-term goals and reaching them was Kurt's model. He stayed connected with his therapist and he remained in constant contact with those who attended the MLM Healthy Heart Association . . . building a strong heart, one step at a time. Not everyone will see the necessity of having a healthy heart. Many of them will not accept the invitation, and say "no." But for every "no" there's a "yes." People who want to prevent an MLM heart attack will do what it takes to get in shape. The exercise regimen is simple: set up a dream, determine the levels, create small goals, map out a strategy, establish realistic expectations, and book the presentations.

Over time, the people who joined the Healthy Heart Association stopped focusing on the material and started focusing on the person, Kurt. He was the living testimony who had recovered from an MLM heart attack, and if he could do it so could they. Kurt made it fun. It didn't seem like physical therapy anymore; it was an exercise to reach a dream.

Dr. Kay wanted Kurt to meet other great doctors and therapists, and for him to share his story, so she invited Sandy and Kurt to a Healthy Heart seminar in Las Vegas. Kurt had just returned to work and getting three days off was a challenge, but he agreed to go.

ELEVEN

It Ends in Vegas

The tires skidded on the pavement as the 747 touched down at the Las Vegas airport. Kurt and Sandy were extremely excited about the conference. Dr. Kay and Dr. McCarty were keynote speakers, as well as a host of others who were successful leaders in preventing MLM heart attacks.

The conference registration response from numerous doctors, therapists, specialists, directors, sponsors and prospects was over 7,000. The airport was jammed with interested people from all over the US and 47 countries that shared a common interest in building a home-based business that promoted healthy living and methods for successful lifestyles.

Kurt and Sandy checked into their hotel, scoped out the lobby of the hotel/casino and the restaurant. After they were settled into their room, they made their way to the Las Vegas Convention Center to obtain their badges and look at the booths from other organizations that were participating in the conference.

Kurt and Sandy were looking at all the books, CDs, DVDs and pamphlets when his cell phone rang. Kurt looked at the caller ID and saw that it was Dr. Kay.

"Hello!" Kurt said with the sound of excitement in his voice.

"Yeah, Kurt, did you and Sandy have a good flight?" she asked.

"Yes, we did. . . And you?" he replied.

"I did, thanks for asking. Have you two gotten settled in yet?"

"Oh, yes, Sandy and I are at the convention center now. Wow! I've never seen so many books and materials in one place. This is amazing," Kurt announced.

"I'm so excited for you and Sandy. You're going to love it. These conventions really motivate and educate people like you, who want their business to grow. Tonight's session is going to be incredible," Dr. Kay emphasized. "The keynote speaker is a single mom who started her MLM healthy heart business and now is a self-made millionaire with thousands of sponsors in her downline. In fact, she has one of the largest networks and many of her sponsors have been awarded a Mercedes Benz for their work and efforts. And Kurt, you're close to winning a Mercedes for your efforts as well."

"Really? No way!" Kurt said. He quickly covered the phone and told Sandy about the keynote speaker and the incentive for the Mercedes cars. Incidentally, the keynote speaker is the same woman who Sandy and Kurt listened to in the car ride home from physical therapy, shortly after Kurt started his physical therapy sessions with Dr. Kay.

"That's right, Kurt. This is more than making money. It's about helping people, building relationships, and giving the opportunity for people to live a happy, healthy, and successful life."

"I can't believe we are here; thank you, Dr. Kay for inviting us," Kurt said with great humility.

"You're welcome, Kurt. You and Sandy are doing so much, and I believe you have the potential to become a great therapist," Dr. Kay said.

"Oh, I don't know . . . I'm just a cop who had an MLM heart attack and wants others to know how to avoid going through what I did," Kurt replied.

"Kurt, you're already a therapist . . . you just demonstrate the physical therapy sessions in hotels and in your home. That's what's so great about this business. Anyone can do it from anywhere," she said.

"Wow, I never thought if it like that," Kurt said.

"I'm on my way to the Convention Center and will arrive in about five minutes," Dr. Kay informed, "I coming down the strip right now. Wait for me near the north entrance and I'll take you in. I have some great seats reserved for you."

"I don't know how to thank you, Dr. Kay," Kurt said.

"You already have," she answered. "See you in a few."

"Okay, goodbye," Kurt replied. He hung up and told Sandy what all Dr. Kay said. They were both beside themselves with anticipation and expectation.

Kurt and Sandy connected with Dr. Kay. She showed them around the exhibits and then took them to their location in the meeting hall. They had great seats on the main floor, center stage.

Kurt and Sandy were in awe of the massive size and decor of the building. The Las Vegas Convention Center is one of the largest and best-equipped convention centers in the U.S. With over 3.2 million square feet of flexible meeting and trade show space and state-of-the-art audio and visual equipment, it's the facility of choice for many top U.S. conventions.

Only ten minutes until the main event was to begin. The stage help were conducting last minute sound checks. Kurt and Sandy watched like kids in a candy shop. That's about when Kurt started to feel ill.

"Kurt, are you all right?" Sandy asked.

Kurt's complexion was white, and he started rubbing his forehead as if he had a headache.

"I should have eaten something before we left the hotel. I was just so excited to get here I didn't give it much thought," Kurt replied. He adjusted his position on the chair trying to get comfortable.

"Did you take your medication?" Sandy asked.

"Not my afternoon pill," he answered.

"I have some in my purse . . . do you want to take it now?"

"Yeah, I guess so. I really shouldn't on an empty stomach, but what choice do I have?"

"Do you want to slip out and get a snack in the lobby?" Sandy asked as she dug into her purse for Kurt's meds.

"No, it's about to start and I don't want to miss a thing," he said.

Sandy handed Kurt bottled water and two pills.

Just then, an announcer took the podium and greeted the crowd.

"Is anybody excited to be in Las Vegas?" the anchor asked.

The crowd cheered with a roar and clapped their hands in a thundering applause. The atmosphere was electric. Kurt and Sandy stood and turned to view the hall. It was packed. Kurt had only seen that many people at a Cubs or White Sox baseball game, but never in a setting like this.

A number of the keynote speakers and leaders of the organization made their way from behind the curtain and took their positions on the left side of the stage. The crowd roared even more when they made their entrance on the platform.

As the conference continued, Kurt and Sandy saw several people receive recognition and reward for their efforts. Several individuals shared their story . . . how they entered the business and what it had done in their lives. Each time a couple or person completed their story everyone stood and cheered.

Sandy looked over to Kurt and smiled, excited in the moment. Kurt was perspiring on his forehead, and his hair around his ears was soaked in sweat.

"Kurt, are you okay?" Sandy asked in deep concern.

"I'll be fine," he responded. Kurt didn't turn to look at Sandy when he answered her. He just stared straight ahead at the stage, smiled and celebrated with the crowd as the last person completed their testimonial.

The keynote speaker was introduced. The audience shouted and applauded as she came to the podium.

"Thank you. . . Thank you very much," she replied.

People remained standing and continued to applaud.

Finally, the keynote speaker motioned her hands for the people to be seated and the spectators sat down.

"It's an honor for me to be on this stage tonight. It was not too many years ago, I was sitting in a meeting similar to this in Phoenix, anticipating my business to grow. No one believed I could do it. I was a single mom, raising my daughters, trying to build a business. But when

I discovered it was more than a business, it was my family . . . things began to change.

"Now I am standing here before you amazed as to what has happened. Sometimes I just want to pinch myself in the morning when I wake up . . . to be sure this is real. I am so grateful."

The crowd laughed in response to her humility and meek approach.

"I am completely unemployable," she said.

The laughter roared aloud.

"With everything that is going on with the economy and financial struggles for businesses and unemployment, it amazes me that people are still looking for a job or a boss, limiting their future to someone else's decisions and judgment.

"We live in challenging times, but there has never been a better time to build and own your own business and be self-employed like now.

"For me, I kind of stumbled upon my opportunity. I grew up in Wisconsin, in a blue-collar family . . . no one in my family went to college, so by default, I followed in that pattern. I was a swimmer, so I went on to become a swim instructor and coach at the high school and college level. And as a swimming coach, I didn't do it for the money, but for the passion of the sport.

"I enjoyed what I was doing, but in the back of my mind, I was looking for something else that could sustain me. When I joined my current business, I was a single mom of three children, ages 5, 7 and 9, with no child support or outside resource helping me. It was entirely up to me to provide for them.

"Now, I'm telling you this so you can understand what kind of stress I was under. And when you are under this type of stress, it can have a positive or negative effect upon you. I call it the two keys: stress can paralyze you or propel you. I chose to let it propel me because I was more interested in what I wanted than what I didn't want.

"I wanted to be there for my children when they got home from school and be there during summer vacation. It was a struggle at first. Many meals were peanut butter sandwiches. And the car I drove was an old beater that took three tries before it would start."

The crowd laughed. Sandy chuckled and looked at Kurt for his reaction. The noise startled Kurt. When Sandy turned, his head was down on his chest and the crowd's reaction alerted Kurt. The medication and the long flight made Kurt tired and he was apparently falling asleep.

Kurt looked at Sandy and gave her an "I'm sorry" look.

The speaker continued with her story, "I kept my head high, because I knew what my dreams were and believed I could make it.

"I look back, some 23 years, and can see that I made some key decisions as a young woman that made the difference . . . and that is what I want to share with you this evening."

Sandy opened her notebook to take notes.

"I started with no money. But with what little I did earn, the first thing I did was to hire an assistant who came over one day a week to help me manage my business. That way, I could be out there showing the plan and building a residual income. As money increased, my assistant's hours increased.

"Next, I hired someone to come and clean my house every week. I really couldn't afford it, but I squeezed it in. I knew that it was more profitable for me to build my business than to clean my home."

Once again, the audience laughed in response to the speaker's story and candid approach.

Sandy looked at Kurt for his reaction, but he was asleep.

"Kurt," Sandy whispered with no response. "Kurt," she said a little louder, but soft enough to not draw attention to herself or to Kurt's condition. She called his name a third time, then nonchalantly bumped him with her elbow, but still no response.

The speaker continued as Sandy contemplated how she was going to wake Kurt without making a scene. She was afraid to bump him again, lest he not wake up and stumble out of his chair. After all, they were front and center. It was something that would not be easy to disguise or hide.

Looking straight ahead, she covered her mouth and directed her voice toward him as she tried again. "Kurt," she whispered. Sandy paused for a moment and then glanced in his direction out of the corner of her eye. Kurt was out for the count like a knocked out boxer.

Please, Kurt, wake up, she murmured to herself.

Sandy was focusing on Kurt when suddenly the speaker spooked her composed efforts to wake him up. Sandy turned forward in the direction of the podium expecting the keynote speaker to be staring directly toward Kurt, when she said, "It's time to wake up! . . ."

Sandy took a deep breath, but was relieved that that comment was not directed at Kurt, but in the context of her speech.

". . . The United States was founded on an entrepreneurial foundation, and we've gotten away from that. We have to get back to our roots. The days of working a job for 30 years for a solid retirement is more difficult now than ever in our history as a nation. The American dream is being shattered by debt and low-paying jobs. Think of this — more than 26 million people are either unemployed or underemployed."

Sandy looked over at Kurt. She was beginning to worry. Normally, Kurt was a light sleeper. The slightest noise in the house and he was wide-awake. She knew that he had skipped dinner and was beginning to think, *maybe his sugar is low . . . wow, he looks so pale. Please don't pass out on me, Kurt. . . oh my God, is he even breathing?*

She looked to make sure. She was getting concerned and began to look around to see what would be the quickest and least obvious route to exit the arena.

Sandy decided to insert her hand into his, and progressively squeeze Kurt's hand and call his name.

"Kurt," she said.

Sandy squeezed harder. "Kurt."

Sandy put her arm around his neck to steady his position so she could jerk his body and squeeze his hand at the same time.

"Kurt? Kurt?" Sandy called, "Kurt, wake up. KURT!"

Suddenly, Kurt jerked. He threw both of his arms down to his sides and grasped for air, as if he was drowning in a pool of water.

Kurt woke up. He looked straight up and there stood Sandy.

"Where's Dr. McCarty?" Kurt asked.

TWELVE

Back to Reality

Sandy stared back into Kurt's eyes. It had been three days since Kurt's surgery and he never regained consciousness, until now. Kurt was heavily medicated and the doctors told her that when he came to, not to expect him to remember much and that one of the side effects of his medication was headaches and the possibility for hallucinations — but not to worry, it would cause no permanent brain damage.

Sandy leaned over the side railing of his bed to slide her fingers through Kurt's hair.

"Hey, baby," Sandy said in a soft, gentle, comforting voice, "how are you feeling?"

"Pretty stupid," Kurt answered.

"What . . . why?" she replied.

"You know, for falling asleep on the front row . . . I'm so sorry. But I'll make it up to you. We can still get tickets," Kurt said.

"Tickets?" she asked.

"I know how bad you wanted to see Celine Dion, and I'll gladly take you," Kurt announced.

"Baby, you just need to rest," she remarked.

"I'm fine . . . let's go see the show and hit some slots. After all, how often do we get to be in Caesar's Palace?" Kurt said.

"What?" Sandy said in bewilderment. "Kurt," she continued, "Dr. McConnell said the medication would cloud your thoughts, so let's just get through this first and. . ."

Kurt interrupted Sandy, "Where's Dr. McCarty? He can explain everything,"

"Your doctor is Dr. McConnell and he. . ."

"No, my doctor is Dr. McCarty . . . the heart surgeon. Go ask the nurse, she'll call for him," Kurt insisted as he pointed toward the door in reference to the nurses' station. When he did, he cringed with pain in his left shoulder.

Kurt continued to beg Sandy to summon Dr. McCarty and no matter how hard she tried, she could not make any headway with him. She didn't know what to anticipate when Kurt woke up, but this was unexpected and more than she could handle. Sandy could not get a word in edgewise. Kurt was verbally persistent, which prevented her from explaining what had occurred over the past few days.

By now, the commotion reached the nurses' station and the head nurse, Kelly, came in to see what was going on.

"Mrs. Dungy, is everything okay?" Kelly asked as she worked her way to view Kurt's monitoring device. Calmly, she evaluated the IV tubes and assessed Kurt's vitals. His blood pressure and heart rate were slightly enhanced, but nothing serious.

Sandy watched Kelly appraise the monitor. Sandy wanted to explain to Kurt what was going on, but his erratic behavior caused her to hesitate for fear how he would react.

When Kelly turned around, she saw the look on Sandy's face. It was sheer panic.

"Let me call Dr. McConnell," Kelly said.

"How many times do I have to say it . . . Dr. McCarty, he's my doctor," Kurt replied. Kurt tried to sit up when he responded, but a sharp pain pierced through his thigh that sent him right back into his bed.

As soon as Kelly left the room, two male nurses came in. They also went straight to Kurt's monitor and IV tubes. They were able to calm Kurt down, which calmed Sandy down as well.

Sandy took a deep breath and looked at the clock. 7:12.

It was Tuesday evening, two days after Easter Sunday. Kurt had been rushed to the hospital early Saturday morning for a gunshot wound with a robbery in progress. His protective vest saved his life. He took two rounds the chest, one in the leg, (nearly hitting a major artery) and one in his shoulder. His fall to the pavement was brutal. He cracked his skull, causing hemorrhaging and minor swelling to his rear lobe. The doctors intentionally medicated him heavily to monitor his brain. He had been unconscious since his surgery.

Kurt calmed down. Sandy pulled up a chair by his bed. He was still confused about his surroundings and because Kurt was talking so irrationally, Sandy decided it was best for Dr. McConnell to explain his injuries and condition.

About twenty minutes went by before Dr. McConnell entered the room.

"Hello Kurt, I'm Dr. McConnell."

"Where's Dr. McCarty?" Kurt responded.

"McCarty? We don't have anyone by that name on staff at this hospital," the doctor said.

"What? That's impossible. He's my heart doctor."

Dr. McConnell turned to Sandy, "Does he see a cardiologist?"

"No," she answered.

"Yes, I do. . . . Look here, I'll prove it!" Kurt pulled his covers over his hips and then pulled up his gown to show his surgical incision from his by-pass surgery. But there was no scar. And, when he did, his shoulder bothered him with an intense throbbing and he subsided.

"Kurt," Dr. McConnell said, explaining his condition, "you've just been through a traumatic event. You've been heavily medicated intentionally to allow us to monitor your brain. You've suffered a concussion, mild hemorrhaging in your brain, and you were shot."

"Shot!" Kurt exclaimed.

"The suspect you were chasing in the alley shot you," Sandy explained.

"You hit your head . . . hard . . . on the pavement. I don't expect you to remember. Your short-term memory is altered, and we will continue to monitor your brain, but for now, you aren't going to remember anything from the other morning," the doctor said.

"I don't get it. Where am I?" Kurt asked.

"The hospital," Sandy answered.

"I know — which one?" Kurt replied.

"Roseland Community," Dr. McConnell responded.

"They have one of these in Vegas too?" Kurt said.

Sandy turned and looked at Dr. McConnell and whispered, "He thinks he's in Las Vegas."

"It's just going to take a little time," the doctor told Sandy, "and some rest."

Sandy, standing beside Kurt's bed, reached down and grabbed Kurt's hand as the doctor informed her that they would monitor his progress and to hope for the best.

"I'll be back in the morning to check on you," Dr. McConnell said and then left the room.

Kurt looked tired, and Sandy tried to convince him to go back to sleep, but that's when Kurt started in.

He told Sandy a detailed account and elaborate story. He shared about how he had suffered an MLM heart attack and had bypass surgery. He told Sandy the story concerning his out-of-body experience. And with deep emotion, he told how he died and what a mess it made for her and the kids. He described Bryan's trouble with the law and being placed in a boy's home. He shared how Lorrie withdrew and developed an online relationship with a boy in Louisville, and then purchased a ticket and while at the bus station, she had a severe allergic reaction and died.

It was quite a story, indeed.

Sandy sat there patiently, listening to every word as Kurt shared how a Dr. McCarty and Dr. Kay Donaldson helped Kurt recover from his MLM heart attack and assist him with a strategy to build his network marketing business, the Healthy Heart Association, as Kurt called it.

Sandy didn't interrupt him for two reasons. First, the ideas and concepts for restarting Kurt's business were great suggestions. Second, it was obvious that Kurt's paralleled presentation and metaphoric analogy concerning Multi-level Marketing and a heart attack were so real to him, she didn't know how to convince him that it was all part of a dramatic mental illusion resulting from medication and his injuries. However, regardless of how far-fetched his epiphany was, for Kurt, it was reality.

Kurt continued to explain his setbacks, physical therapy, how he started implementing the concepts he learned from reading books and listening to CDs, the growth of the business, and hosting large meetings in hotels. It was a fascinating narrative, mixed with bits and pieces of realism, fiction, fantasy, and metaphors.

Sandy was amazed. Kurt had only been conscious for less than an hour, and yet his vivid explanation was filled with so many reasonable reflections and practical procedures. She wished she had a notebook to write it all down before Kurt forgot his chronicle. *This would make a great book*, Sandy thought to herself as Kurt chronologically unfolded his "supposed" life story account.

His story was so compelling; Sandy was mesmerized by Kurt's enthusiasm. *Maybe this experience will help Kurt restart his MLM business*, Sandy pondered.

Kurt continued, "Then, Dr. Kay invited us to a motivational conference in Las Vegas. It was huge. Thousands of sponsors, leaders, doctors, therapists and successful entrepreneurs gathered in the Las Vegas Convention Center. And the hotel . . . unbelievable, Sandy. . . just you and I, we were so excited to be there we left the hotel without eating dinner.

"Shortly after we arrived at the convention center, we met Dr. Kay, my therapist, and she got us front row seats!"

"Really," Sandy said with enthusiasm.

"Yeah. . . some of the greatest networkers were there. One of the keynote speakers shared her story . . . and that's when it happened."

"What happened, Kurt."

"I fell asleep."

"You what?" Sandy said, trying not to laugh.

"I was tired from the flight, we didn't eat before we left the hotel and when I took my heart medication, it made me sleepy."

"I see," Sandy replied.

"So, I can't remember what happened after that. . . How long have we been back from Vegas? I don't remember going back to work. And how did I get shot? Since my heart attack, I've been assigned office duty, so when did I go back on the beat?"

"Kurt, you never had a heart attack, nor have we been to Las Vegas," Sandy said. She waited and watched to see how he would react to her candid statement.

"Then how did I get this scar?" he said pointing to his chest.

"Kurt, you have no scar," Sandy said.

Kurt reached down to lift his gown to view his chest. Sandy assisted him so he could get a good look.

"See, no scar," Sandy said.

"Shut the front door!" Kurt responded.

Kurt leaned his head back onto his pillow in disbelief.

"Kurt, you've been unconscious for over three days and apparently, your subconscious mind merged all your thoughts and created a story-line of events that appear very real to you right now. But none of that happened."

Kurt reached over with his left hand, attempting to lift his shirt sleeve, but his bullet wound in his shoulder prevented him from doing so. In frustration, he dropped his head back onto his pillow and sighed with irritation.

"What are you trying to do?" Sandy asked.

"Look at my tattoo," he answered.

"Kurt you don't have a tattoo. . . Do you?" she replied.

"Yeah, on my right bicep."

Sandy walked around to the other side of the bed and lifted his sleeve, but there was nothing there. Kurt was disappointed . . . not because the tattoo was not there, but because his tale was just a dream. *Back to reality*, Kurt thought to himself.

Kurt's demeanor and countenance instantly changed. He not only looked very tired, but also he looked depressed.

"Kurt," Sandy responded. "This is a good thing," she added.

"Really . . . what's good about it?"

"Kurt, your story might not be real, but the things you told me about what you learned to restart and grow your network marketing business were incredible. We need to reconnect with Randy and share this with him."

Randy Whitcomb was Kurt's upline sponsor for his MLM business and since they moved, Kurt disconnected with Randy and stopped returning his calls. Frankly, Kurt was avoiding him like the plague.

"If we share this story, Randy will think I'm crazy." Kurt paused for a moment, "I think it's crazy."

"I don't think it's crazy, and you're not crazy either," Sandy reassured.

"This sucks," Kurt replied.

"What sucks?" Sandy asked.

"We were so close to winning a Mercedes and now. . ."

"But think of it," Sandy interjected, "I know it was just a dream, but with Randy's help, and what you experienced in your vision, your dream can become *the* dream . . . and then a reality. Who knows, maybe this happened for a purpose."

"Ya think so?" Kurt responded.

"Yes, I do. Here's what we're gonna do," Sandy said excitedly, "I want you to get a good night's sleep, then tomorrow morning, I'll bring a recorder, and I want you to tell me your story . . . leaving nothing out, no matter how crazy it seems . . . and I'll take it home and type it out in its entirety. That way we have it in writing. We can start over, but this time with more insight and knowledge. You know what Randy always says, 'knowledge is power.'"

Sandy looked up at the clock on the wall . . . 9:39.

"It's late, and I need to get back to the kids," she said.

"Who's watching them?" Kurt asked.

"My mother."

Kurt rolled his eyes. He loved his mother-in-law, but from a distance.

"She's just here to help for a few days so I could be here with you. I've haven't left your side one day . . . I was waiting for you to wake up." Her voice cracked, her emotions took over and she began to cry.

Kurt quickly responded to her emotion, "I love you, baby."

"I love you, too," Sandy said with a smile as a tear rolled down her cheek. Kurt smiled back.

"Everything is going to work out, you'll see," Sandy said.

THIRTEEN

Revisit the Dream

The next morning Sandy drove to the hospital with her recorder, ready to document Kurt's vision. She pondered his tale all night, tossing and turning in bed, envisioning the potential and possibilities of a life change. Even though Kurt seemed frustrated that his vision wasn't real and that he'd been unconscious for three days, Sandy was convinced that this encounter was a wakeup call.

The detail in Kurt's account was astonishing. Despite the fact his recall of names was limited or vague, the specifics in other areas were remarkable, namely, the titles of books he'd read, the content from CDs and the instruction from Dr. McCarty and Dr. Kay. What was even more amazing was the unique parallel between Kurt's heart attack and its allegorical use within the network marketing industry.

MLM heart attack . . . CPR . . . Healthy Heart Association . . . what a comparison, where'd he come up with that? Sandy thought. She understood that his mental-metaphoric encounter was a combination of his head injury and the heavy medication, but it still didn't explain the nature or source of his story.

Before Sandy went to bed, she surfed the web and found a couple of books that Kurt said he had read. She had no problem remembering one title, *Beach Money*, and she also found an online bookstore, Next Century Publishing, and ordered two books.

Sandy was a little nervous, wondering how Kurt would react today. *Is he going to be positive or negative? Is he going to be depressed? What if he doesn't want to tell his story again? After all, his last words were, "I'm crazy." Will he feel stupid and not want to participate in sharing his story with Randy? Will he even remember anything the next day? What if he forgot everything and they didn't capture it on recording? What then?*

She played the possible scenarios in her mind and then realized she had to think positive and believe that whatever the outcome, she and Kurt were going to dedicate themselves to restart and build a successful network marketing business.

She was about five minutes out, and it started to rain. She turned on the windshield wipers as it began to pour. The weather change caused her to stop thinking about all her questions and to concentrate on her drive to the hospital.

When she entered Kurt's room, he was sitting up and eating break-fast. He may have lost his memory, but not his appetite. The nurses had already changed his bandages, so there was no denying he had been shot.

"Before we get started," Kurt said as he took another bite of his bacon, "can you tell me what happened that night?"

Sandy knew he was referring to the incident of the shooting.

"According to the police reports and Mike told me. . ."

"Mike?" Kurt asked.

"Mike Shell," Sandy answered.

"Was he there?"

"Yes, he arrived on the scene shortly after shots were fired. Apparently, you were in foot pursuit after one of the two suspects."

"The robbery?" Kurt inquired.

"Yes," Sandy said. She was encouraged that he remembered and was hoping what she shared would bring back his memory.

"Your partner, Jim Coleman, had already apprehended one of the suspects. He handcuffed him and put him in your cruiser. By now, backup arrived for Jim, and other patrol officers were headed your way to cut off the suspect you were chasing. They pulled up to the opposite end of the alley to block him. When they did, he turned around and saw you approaching.

"This part is a little fuzzy because I haven't seen the police report, but apparently, the robber started shooting at you and the other officers shot him."

"They kill him?" Kurt asked.

"No, he's at another hospital. He took one in the back. Of course, he was arrested for larceny, attempted homicide, assault with a deadly weapon and assault on a police officer with bodily injury."

Kurt just sat there . . . silent. The reality of what had happened began to sink in and he realized he could have been killed.

"In the alley, there was a dumpster and some scrap metal on the ground nearby. When you were shot, you fell on a steal beam and cracked your skull. That's why you have the bandage around your head."

"Yeah, the thing drove me crazy last night . . . itchy," Kurt said in reference to the head bandage.

"The ambulances arrived," Sandy continued . . . "it made all the news stations, channels 5, 7, 32, all the major networks. Then we waited and you woke up. End of story. Now, here we are."

"Wow," Kurt said. "How long am I gonna be laid up?"

"Not sure. Dr. McConnell said it could be a couple of days or more, depending on your head injury."

"McConnell . . . McCarty . . . that's freaky," Kurt replied.

"What's freaky?" Sandy asked.

"Their names . . . they're so closely related. Isn't that weird?"

"Yeah, I guess so," she answered. "Hey, you ready to get started?"

"For what?" Kurt inquired.

"To record your story," she answered.

"What story?" Kurt said.

Sandy's eyes enlarged as she looked at Kurt in shock and disbelief. *Oh my gosh*, she thought . . . *he's forgot already.*

Before she had a chance to say anything, Kurt burst out laughing and when he did, it hurt his head. He reached up, placed his hand on the back of his skull and said chuckling, "I'm just kidding." He continued to cackle.

"That's not funny," Sandy remarked.

"If you could have seen the look on your face. . ."

Sandy gave Kurt that look, the look of a wife who was very unhappy.

"Sorry, babe," he said, "I couldn't resist it . . . I mean you walked right into it."

"Okay, very funny . . . now do you think we can be serious?" she replied.

Kurt continued to laugh and after about three seconds, Sandy changed her tune and giggled along.

Just then Dr. McConnell walked in to see the two of them cutting up and laughing.

"Well, somebody's doing much better," the doctor declared.

The explanation was too difficult and lengthy to share, so both Sandy and Kurt chose not to divulge any details pertaining to Kurt's vision.

Dr. McConnell gave a preliminary update. He shared what tests he was going to run and what they were looking for. If everything looked good, Kurt could be released on Sunday or Monday. That was good news and both Sandy and Kurt were optimistic. They thanked the doctor and he left to make his rounds.

Over the next four hours, Kurt shared his story. Sandy listened as the recorder captured his account. They took a break for lunch and then continued until Kurt started to get sleepy. Sandy went home to be with the kids a couple of hours and then returned around 6 o'clock that evening.

Kurt was waiting anxiously to continue telling his story. When Sandy walked in, the nurses were changing one of his IV bags. Once the nurse left, Kurt and Sandy continued recording Kurt's vision. They called it quits at 9:15. Kurt was just beginning to share about the techniques he used to recruit others in joining his Healthy Heart Association, which was really his network marketing business. He stopped when it came to the part where he booked a hotel for his first large group meeting.

"We can finish in the morning, that is if you're not too tired," Sandy said.

"I want to finish this while it's fresh in my mind," Kurt replied.

"Honey, I can't tell you how excited I am," she responded. "Oh yeah, I almost forgot; I found three of the books you told me about yesterday. When I got home last night, I searched for them online. Hope it's all right; I ordered us copies."

"Really? That's great. You're such an awesome wife."

"I know," Sandy said and smiled.

Kurt grinned back, "Crazy girl."

On the drive home, Sandy reminisced the all-day ordeal, Kurt's story and the crucial information for restarting the business. What seemed to be a burden turned out to be a blessing. Somehow, Sandy's sorrow was silenced by Kurt's story and the dream was returning inside of her.

She recalled Kurt and her joking with each other and his prank of forgetting the story. Revisiting it made her laugh out loud. She looked into the rearview mirror. It was still positioned at her face and not the rear window. She had forgotten to readjust it. The last thing she does before she exits the car, as many women do, is to take one last glance inspecting makeup and hair.

She glanced again, and reached up to move it into its drive mode position, but before she did, she smiled thinking about their future. She daydreamed some of Kurt's story becoming a reality. Her fears and concerns for Kurt were fading away. Her giddy feelings were filled with joy and happiness, so much so, she decided to turn on the radio.

When the radio came on, she looked down and noticed that it was on 97.9, WLUP-FM, "The Loop," Chicago's classic rock station.

Bryan, she thought, realizing he changed the station last. She decided not to adjust the station because the song playing fit her mood. The song selection was Boston, *Don't Look Back*. The timing could not have been more appropriate. Sandy turned up the volume and sang the lyrics aloud at the top of her lungs in glee:

Don't look back.

A new day is breakin'

It's been too long since I felt this way

I don't mind where I get taken,
The road is callin'
Today is the day.

Sandy felt like a teenager again, rocking her head to the rhythm and singing as if she was on stage surrounded by thousands of fans. The guitar solo began and she thought, *Kurt would crack up if he saw me now.*

Just then, Sandy's cell phone rang. She didn't hear it at first until there was a quick break between the guitar and the next verse. She turned down the volume and looked at her cell phone screen. The call read, "PRIVATE." She didn't know who it was, and typically, she didn't answer when she didn't recognize the caller. But she thought, *Why not.*

"Hello?"

"Honey."

"Kurt, is everything all right?"

"Yes. I wanted to see if you could go in the garage. I know how bad you hate spiders, so I hesitated asking you."

"What is it?" Sandy replied.

"Can you find my box of pictures? You know the ones we keep on the refrigerator . . . our vision pictures."

"I know right where it is," Sandy said.

"You're awesome, baby," Kurt said.

"I know," Sandy replied and then laughed.

Kurt started laughing too, "The dream is alive! I'm back!"

Sandy and Kurt reconnected as a couple, and it felt good!

FOURTEEN

Vision Speaks

Two weeks had gone by since Kurt was released from the hospital. His mobility was progressing. Ironically, Kurt's bullet wounds were to his left shoulder and his right thigh. This afforded him the ability to use a cane in his right hand, which enabled him to hobble around the house, but his mobility was limited.

Kurt didn't waste any time. The day he was released, he called Randy from the hospital. Kurt briefly shared what had transpired with his injuries, but expressed how he wanted to restart the business. Randy was encouraging and comforting, assuring Kurt he would be there for him. Randy told Kurt to call him after he returned home and he would come and see him, which he did, and they had a grand visit for over two hours. Randy was going out of town for a week. The plan was, when he returned he was going to return for another visit.

Before Randy left, he had Kurt rejoin the team. He stressed the importance to keeping the dream alive and focusing on the future. He asked Kurt what his dreams were. Kurt shared what his goals and desires were.

"Kurt, you've just been through a traumatic event, and I am so excited that you want to restart. Let me ask you; what made you first decide to start in network marketing?"

"I got sick of my job. I needed to get a new job . . . and I wasn't spending any time with my kids," Kurt answered.

"So, seeing that you've been injured, what are your plans now?' Randy asked.

"I am on sick leave for now. But I really want to build my business as fast as I can . . . hopefully, I won't have to return to work for six or seven months."

"Wow," Randy replied, "now that's a big vision."

Kurt laughed, "I know, but I'm being serious."

"I'm sure you are. How much money will it take for you to quit your job?" Randy said.

"Well, before I got shot, I was making $3,800 a month."

"What if you could reach $5,000 a month, could you retire then? Would that excite you?"

"Absolutely!"

"Cool," Randy remarked. "But before we can reach that total, we have to clarify your target points. Let's say five grand is the target. To do that in six months is a difficult thing to do. I am not saying it can't happen, but given your situation, it's not reasonable. So let's be realistic and work on short-term goals. It's more likely that you can reach four to five thousand dollars a month in three to four years."

"But I did it . . ." Kurt started to talk about his vision and decided to drop it. Maybe what he did in his dream was unrealistic and he needed to take it one day at a time.

"Let's make our first target to be $500 a month, and let's say you are going to reach that in five months. Maybe three, but I don't want to push it with your recovery and all."

"Why you trying to handicap me?" Kurt said.

"Okay . . . that's fair. So, let's say you spend ten hours a week for the next 90 days, and at the end of 90 days, we see where you are. If you can reach that goal, you're doing good."

"That works . . . but because I'm on sick leave, I can spend a lot more than ten hours a week."

Randy was trying to keep Kurt's zeal alive, but at the same time, keep him balanced. Next, Randy showed the compensation plan and then they mapped out a specific strategy. Randy stressed the importance of Kurt having specific directions to achieve his goal of $500 a month.

"Once you have the dollar amount, now you need to have a strategy on how to get it. That means what you will do each day, each week, and calculate how much work it will take to reach that target. Got it?" Randy asked.

"Got it," Kurt replied.

"Okay, next we need to start a list of names."

"Like this?" Kurt said as he handed him a stack of paper with names, phone numbers, occupation, and type of relationship they had, if any, to Kurt and Sandy.

Randy took it, looked at the top sheet, paused for a second, and then quickly looked at the remaining sheets. He looked back and Kurt and then Sandy and said, "Holy crap!"

Kurt and Sandy laughed with excitement. They were not trying to impress Randy; they knew that this was something important, and they had never taken the time to make a concrete list. Even with Kurt's recovery in the hospital, they worked on their list every day.

"Man, there must be 300 names here," Randy replied in shock.

"Actually, 347 . . . to be exact," Sandy said.

"For real?" Randy said. "347?"

"Precisely," Sandy said.

"And she entered each name in an Excel file so we can print out reports whenever we need them," Kurt replied.

"This is great," Randy said. "What you need to do is start making calls to make presentations. If we can make six presentations and build it up to 16, then you will see your business start to grow. I don't want you to focus on the $5,000 but on the $500. Focus on your calendar and the meetings. What nights will your do your meetings?"

Sandy opened a day planner. She had the month color-coded. The days for meetings were colored in green. The days they made calls were colored in yellow. And days they made follow-up calls were in red. Sandy wrote three numbers on the meeting days, one for the number of people they would invite, another for how many they expected to show, and another for how many people would accept the presentation.

"This is good. I just don't want you to get discouraged if you don't reach these numbers," Randy said.

"We agree . . . we just want to have goals," Kurt replied.

"That's great. It's a numbers game, simple math," Randy said.

Randy gave them a DVD that showed the presentation. "I want you to watch this as many times as possible. Know it backwards and forward. In your initial meetings, show this DVD. Over time, you will become more familiar and when I feel you are ready, you can give the presentations yourself. But don't worry. I will come to as many meetings as I can to help you get started. You will learn as you watch me."

Randy shared some tips for sharing the presentation, such as making them feel comfortable. Treat them like a friend. Transfer feeling and emotion. Be an encourager and always make eye contact. Randy role played with Kurt and Sandy to show them what to do. He was preparing them so they wouldn't stress out. He gave them material that explained the plan, and the do's and don'ts.

"Kurt, once we've done six or more meetings together, you should have two or three contracts. At that time, I will expect you to know the material and to perform on your own with two or three prospects. I will coach you."

Next, Randy showed Kurt and Sandy five points for how to book their meetings, how to use the calendar and begin the process.

Although Kurt's wounds took some time to heal, his recovery time for his head injury was remarkable. He had no headaches, no memory loss, no blackouts, and no hemorrhaging. Dr. McConnell cautioned Kurt that his medication could instigate mood swings and feelings of depression, but Kurt was doing great.

In fact, the three books Sandy purchased for him while he was in the hospital, he read in just two days. Randy promised to bring him some CDs when he returned. In the mean time, Sandy and Kurt listened to the vision recording three times. They debated with each other, and finally decided to play the recording for Randy the next time he came over. Kurt wasn't afraid anymore about what someone might say or think; it was his dream, and it rekindled hope for him and Sandy.

They got busy making calls and booking people for presentations. They couldn't wait for Randy to return. They had ten meetings scheduled for week one, and 13 meetings for week two. Sandy kept track of the responses, and Kurt made the calls. They had a system worked out, and they did it every day.

Ten days passed, and Randy returned to town. The next night he was back at Kurt and Sandy's home. They gave Randy 10 CDs that contained Kurt's vision recording they did at the hospital. In return, Randy had a box full of nearly 30 CDs and 10 DVDs for Kurt and Sandy to listen to and view.

They showed Randy their calendar and the number of presentations scheduled. He was impressed with their ambition and passion for the industry.

"This is a great start," Randy said. "But what I want you to remember is that building your business is 90% relationships and 10% mechanics."

Sandy looked at Kurt, and Kurt looked at Sandy. They just grinned.

"What it is?" Randy asked in response to their reaction.

"Oh, nothing," Kurt replied. "Go on."

"It's about relationship building. It's not so much about selling the company, the products, or even the benefits of owning your own business. It's about YOU!

"It's about first impressions. How do you present yourself?" Randy enforced.

Randy reached into his black, leather briefcase and retrieved a book, *How to Win Friends and Influence People* by Dale Carnegie.

"I know that you've probably read this before, but read it again.

"Kurt, people skills are powerful. I feel that your previous attempts to develop your business failed because you didn't cultivate relationships with your downline. How we communicate, the things we say, the tone of our voice, a positive reinforcement, and remembering someone's name are all crucial techniques that reveal we genuinely care about people.

"Even the top earners in our company stress the importance of continuously developing good people skills. It's posturing a positive attitude. You need to incorporate these skills. Everyone's personality is different and no two individuals are alike. But, regardless of how you do your presentations, it is vital to remember this; make people feel valuable. Winning is in the relationship building, not the products.

"I have met many salespersons who know their products and the plan inside out, but no one is attracted to a know-it-all. These types of people don't succeed, because within minutes after meeting a prospect, they try to sell their product without cultivating a relationship.

"And another thing . . . there are some do's and don'ts when it comes to prospecting. For instance, I've heard you say this in the past . . . 'I called so and so told them about a business opportunity but they didn't show up to the presentation.'

"Kurt, that's not going to work. There's a saying that says, 'Less is more.' Sharing too much information only feeds questions. You want to feed curiosity not questions. It's important that you control perception. It's not what you say, but what they think you are saying that is so important. You have to control the conversation.

"If a person asks you, 'What do I have to do?' or 'How much does it cost?' Don't answer them before you get them to the presentation. Say something like this, 'That's a great question . . . and I'm sure you will have plenty more. Take this DVD,' or if you are going to use our website, say, 'Write down this website address. It will answer a lot of questions.'"

"I gotcha," Kurt said.

"Kurt, unfortunately, many make this mistake. Now, I'm not suggesting you avoid questions, be rude, or be evasive. I'm simply saying that your answers should always keep you in the driver's seat. Don't make the assumption that many questions mean the person is highly interested, which causes you to overreact. Stay calm and collected; your goal is to get them to see your presentation.

"Also, don't get frustrated with your prospect if they ask questions. We live in a knowledge society. People will ask questions. But again, Kurt, sharing too much too soon is a bad thing. Think of it like this — high school teachers and college instructors reserve a question and answer time for after the lecture and not before.

"What's most important is letting them know you care. Your enthusiasm will motivate them to *want* to know *what* you know. Showing that you care will open the door to scheduling a time to make a presentation.

If they can feel your passion, then you can say, 'I have some time this week, will Tuesday or Wednesday work for you?' Giving them options is better. It increases your odds of making that appointment."

Sandy was taking notes and Kurt was listening intently. Randy continued to share the basics to prospecting and tips for success in making their presentations. Kurt was soaking it all up like a sponge.

After about an hour of discussion, they took a break and made their way to the kitchen nook. Sandy had prepared strawberry shortcake. They sat at the table drinking coffee as Kurt shared how excited he was and his disinterest in his police job.

Randy gave them a strategy and a plan of attack.

"Okay, now for that list of names. It's a numbers game, as you know. The same is true in any sales company. The more people you talk to, the greater the number who will accept the invitation.

"Once you acquire two or three people, then we will mentor and train them on how to do what you do. It's a ripple effect. I'm telling you, Kurt, if you can find some people who have half as much drive as you two do, you will blow this thing up!"

That excited Kurt, "For real!"

"But here's the key. Don't focus on the "no's." A "no" is not a "no," it's a 'this is not for me.' For every twenty "no's," there's one "yes." And two or three "yeses" can change everything!

"Consistency and urgency are paramount. Now that you have a strategy that works for you, determine how many hours per week you are going to work the business. In those hours, how many calls will you make? From your calls, how many appointments will you secure? Work the system. Don't deviate from the plan. Make your calls and expect results.

"And remember, you're only shooting for your small targets. A small goal obtained is better than a large target missed."

"Sounds like a plan," Kurt said seriously.

"You guys ready to rock Chicago?" Randy asked with enthusiasm.

"We sure are," Sandy said as she stood up from the kitchen table.

Randy shook Kurt's hand and gave Sandy a light hug.

"Call me . . . I'm here for you guys," Randy said as he stood at the front door, about to exit their home.

They shut the door. Kurt stood there with his cane in hand. "You ready for this?"

"I'm ready," Sandy affirmed.

Sandy cleaned the kitchen while Kurt sat in the den reading over Sandy's notes and reading what she wrote from tonight's meeting. He skimmed the pages and when he saw "90% relationships and 10% mechanics," he noticed Sandy had written something in the margin beside it . . . "The VISION speaks!"

Kurt laughed to himself thinking about his dream. "Honey," he called to the kitchen.

"Yes," Sandy said.

"The vision speaks!"

FIFTEEN

Meet the Mentor

Two days had passed since Randy visited. Sandy and Kurt were busy listening to CDs and watching the DVDs that Randy gave them. Kurt read the books, *How to Win Friends and Influence People*, *90 Days to Success* and *How to Build a Multi-Level Money Machine*. He actually took notes, which surprised Sandy; Kurt wasn't much for reading or writing, he mostly watched sports. But since he had come home from the hospital, he had not watched one baseball game or tuned into ESPN. That in itself was a miracle.

Kurt and Sandy were sitting at the kitchen table, going over their calendar and the prospect printout that provided them statistical information on their progress, when the phone rang.

Sandy looked at the caller ID and handed the phone to Kurt, "It's Randy."

"Hello," Kurt said.

"Hey, Kurt . . . how are you doing?"

"Doing well."

"I'm calling for two reasons. First, I wanted to tell you that I've listened to six of the CDs you gave me. That story is amazing."

"Thank you, Randy, that means a lot coming from you."

Randy was not only Kurt's upline, but he was a prominent leader in their network marketing business. He had hundreds, if not a thousand, people in his downline. Kurt was humbled that he would spend so much time with him. Their relationship was stronger now than it was when Kurt first joined a year and a half ago, mostly because Randy intimidated Kurt, and he felt he let him down by not succeeding. So, Kurt avoided him and didn't stick with the system or follow his advice.

"Now let's get this straight. This all happened while you were unconscious for three days after your accident?"

"Yes, sir," Kurt answered formally as he converted into cop mode.

"Where did you get this stuff?" Randy asked.

"I don't understand the question," Kurt replied, answering his question like a detective.

"Had you ever been in the hospital for a heart condition?"

"No."

"Do you know anyone who has had heart trouble or a heart attack?"

"No."

"Is anyone in your family a doctor, a nurse, or a surgeon?"

"No," Kurt replied. He was beginning to lose the feeling of gratitude and become anxious, as if Randy was questioning the validity of his story.

"I'm telling you, I've never heard anything like this before. This stuff is off the chain," Randy's voice inflection projected a positive approval, which allowed Kurt to relax a bit.

Randy continued to praise Kurt, "I mean, the analogy between the business and the heart . . . it's pure genius."

"Thank you," Kurt reiterated.

"Have you given this to anyone else?" Randy inquired.

"No, why?" Kurt asked.

"Because I have a friend in Canada who has a publishing company and I would like to share it with him and see what he thinks."

"Really!" Kurt said with a high-pitch of excitement.

"What did he say?" Sandy asked.

Kurt covered the phone and whispered, "He knows a publisher in Canada . . . he loves the story . . . he's listened to half of it and loves it!"

Sandy put her hands on her hips and said, "See, I told ya."

"That's what Sandy said," Kurt replied, knowing he had to give her credit, especially because she just reminded him of what she said in the hospital.

"Listen, I have a friend, actually he's my mentor . . . and he is coming to Chicago next week. I would like him to meet you and Sandy," Randy said.

"Sure," Kurt replied, somewhat in shock.

"Okay, I'll get more information and get back to you."

"Sounds great," Kurt answered.

"Here's what I'm thinking; I want to listen to the rest of the CDs and . . . with your permission, I would like to share some of your story with my mentor."

"Alright."

Kurt was grinning from ear to ear. Sandy stepped close to where Kurt was sitting and leaned down to hear the conversation.

"Hold on a second . . . Hold on a second . . ." Kurt told Randy. He removed his cell phone from his ear and put it on speaker so Sandy could hear.

"Okay, go ahead Randy."

"Second, my mentor is my guest tonight on the conference call line, and is going to do about fifteen to twenty minutes of teaching. Do you still have the conference number and access code?"

"I do."

"Great, it's at 8:30 central standard time."

"Can't wait," Kurt said.

"Awesome. Yeah, you guys are going to do great, and again, this stuff is awesome . . . I love it . . . MLM heart attack, now that's catchy," Randy said and then started chuckling.

Randy asked a few questions as to their prospect calls and appointment times. Sandy spoke up and gave him a quick update as to their progress. Randy checked his schedule on his phone and typed in the dates for the next two meetings to be held at Kurt's house. Randy gave a two-minute pep talk and the call ended.

At 8:28, Sandy made sure Kurt had his phone. He was sitting in the den, reading over his notes from the book he just finished reading.

"It's about that time," Sandy said.

Kurt called the conference line, entered the access code and then activated the speakerphone.

After waiting for about a minute, Randy came on the call to address the listeners. He greeted everyone, shared some highlights of upcoming events and new videos on the website, and then introduced the keynote speaker.

"I am really excited tonight . . . everybody, we have a special treat tonight . . . one of the top money earners in the company, a man who's made hundreds of millions in the business is our guest tonight. He lives in Los Angeles, and in that city alone, he has 7.2 percent of the city in his downline. It's my honor to give to you my mentor and friend, Denny Harris."

"Thank you, Randy, for that introduction. It is a privilege to speak to you tonight. Randy has told me so much about many of you that are out there building your business, making your calls, booking meetings and showing the plan to prospects. We have a great system and if you follow it closely, it will work for you as it did for me.

"Many of you know my testimony, but for those of you who do not, I was in two network marketing companies before joining our company. At the age of 19, I was excited to see the potential in this industry. Network marketing has provided an opportunity for me and my wife to help thousands of people reach their potential and accomplish their dreams.

"Before I was 30 years old, I become a multi-millionaire. Currently my business has over 250,000 people in my city alone, not counting the U.S. and foreign countries.

"I want to take a few minutes tonight to share with you some secrets to building a successful team in your MLM business. We all know that without a strong team you won't raise to the top. And sponsoring people is one of the most challenging aspects to this type of business. For some, recruiting, training, leading and supporting individuals in this business comes naturally. But for people like me, it doesn't come naturally.

"There is a lot more to building a successful team than just sponsoring people into your business. Real quickly, because I know your time is precious, I want to share five keys to building a team.

"Number one . . . Make a commitment. Most people would agree that they would prefer an equity position to a job. That's means, say goodbye to your boss. Also, most people would prefer a steady income source for financial freedom. That's the American dream right there in a nutshell.

"But nearly 95 percent of Americans never reach this goal and the five percent who do, don't get there overnight. It's a process, and you will never reach your dream without a commitment. Sure, this business is a blast and exciting things can happen, but there are also some lean times.

"I can remember when I lived off Ramen noodles for months at a time. For those of you who don't know what Ramen noodles are, you aren't missing much, I can promise you that. In other words, there will also be tough times, and if you do it long enough, you will have some failures along the way. Don't let it stop you on your journey!

"When a person gets into this business, he should commit to building the business for no less than a year. Most people give up right before they're about to reach the success they've been working for; don't be one of them. Focus on building your business, avoid distractions from other people and other opportunities, and resist obstacles. Consistent daily actions toward the growth and success will build your business and a successful team.

"Number two . . . Learn all you can. In order to build a successful team, you must increase your knowledge about the business you're involved with and how it works. It's almost impossible to know all the answers or successfully train others unless you understand the system and strategies of your business.

"Watch the training and orientation videos on the company's website and be sure to view all of the training materials. Every month, we put up new videos. Take advantage of them. If you want to build your business, absorb all the information you can so people will see you as an expert, as a leader, and they will follow your example.

"Number three . . . Be the Model Sponsor. As a sponsor, you need to be a guide, a trainer, and a supporter. To provide the right kind of leadership to your team, be the type of sponsor that you wish you had. Now, that doesn't mean your current sponsor is a dud. What I mean is, no matter what kind you had, be the best one ever.

"It's vital you stay connected to the people you bring into the business and be there for them when they need help. You also need to use the system you received and duplicate that in others in your team. Lead by example, and those whom you train well, will train others as you did them.

"Number four . . . Be a Motivator and an Innovator. Motivation begins with relationships and ends with results. By staying humble, and at the same time, successful, others will want to follow your lead. Make it a point to share success stories balanced with horror stories. In other words, share the dream but remember how you overcame the obstacles.

"Being an innovator means you take the leadership role and responsibility. That means you must always be positive and encouraging. Build up your team with accolades and praises. To focus or emphasize on the negatives, worries, and complaints will hinder the growth of your team. Everything flows from the top down.

"And number five . . . Empower with TNT. TNT stands for tools, networking, training. Besides your personal support, it is important to provide your team with the proper tools. I know that we have depended on tapes and CDs over the years, but I still am a stickler for books. You should ask your upline, sponsor, or mentor what his or her top ten favorite books are that helped build their business. Then pass those titles down to your team.

"In addition to personal growth development tools, network your books, CDs and DVDs. Sharing is just part of developing a successful team. Finally, training . . . it's important that you dial in to the conference calls and attend as many meetings and conferences as possible.

"Maybe you have attended many and feel that there is nothing new. Attending these meetings is a source of training; you can learn from the best and the brightest to become a leader. Someday, you might be the person speaking, and watching others shows you how it's done.

"Using these five keys to build your team will strengthen your confidence and build a successful network marketing business. Randy."

"Wow, that's some great stuff folks. Thank you so much for sharing that tonight, Denny. Awesome! Don't forget people, you can redial the conference line anytime 24/7 and use the access code 652371# and listen to the recording. All recordings remain for thirty days and if you go to the website and click on "Archives" and then select CCT, which stands for Conference Call Training, then select the date you wish to obtain . . . you can download a free copy of that call.

"That's all we have for tonight . . . thanks for tuning in and we will be back next week — same time — same day. Be blessed!"

Sandy stopped her recorder.

"See how it sounds," Kurt requested of Sandy.

She pressed rewind, waiting a minute or so and pressed play. The recording sounded perfect. Kurt had never recorded a call before that night. In fact, many nights he muted ESPN and watched a ball game while tuning in and out between the call and the game. But not tonight. Sandy was so excited. This was not only their first recording, but it was the first time they had listened together.

The incident with Kurt's shooting, the vision unveiling, and the new zeal in the business, combined to put a special spark in their marriage. No longer did they go in separate directions and live separate lives. They had a common goal, a common purpose, and a common dream. Life was good.

Sandy also took notes. She was reading the five keys to Kurt when the phone rang. Sandy looked at the caller ID.

"It's a 310 area code," Sandy said.

"Well it's not a bill collector . . ." Kurt said.

Sandy looked back to see how he would know.

"It's after 9. They can't call after 9, can they?" Kurt replied. "Go ahead, see who it is."

"Hello?" Sandy answered.

"Hi, this is Denny Harris . . . I'm a friend of Randy Whitcomb. I was trying to reach Kurt Dungy. Is this Sandy?"

"Yes, this is Sandy." She quickly covered the phone and said, "It's Denny Harris!"

"What!" Kurt said. He said it so loud . . . Sandy placed one finger to her lips and gave him the "hush sign."

Sandy was so excited. She started pacing immediately, walking up and down the room. She looked like a child who'd just received a call from Santa Claus.

"I heard what your husband went through and that he's recovering very well and behind every good man, there's a great woman."

"Oh, why thank you, Mr. Harris," Sandy said. She was so tickled she even started to blush.

"Oh no, please, call me Denny."

"Yes, sir," she said nervously.

"No, Denny."

"Oh, yes, uh Denny," she stammered.

Denny chuckled having fun and being his normal outgoing self in an attempt to charm Sandy with his generous poise. Denny lived in Los Angeles, but he was originally from Dawson, Georgia, a small town northwest of Albany. His southern drawl was strong, and Sandy recognized his voice immediately after just listening to the conference call.

"Well here's my better half," Sandy said as she handed Kurt the phone.

"Hello . . . Hello . . . Hello?"

Kurt took the phone away from his ear to view the screen. It took a second to ignite the screen on his Android.

"Crap, I think I just hung up on him," Kurt said.

Just then, the phone rang again. It was Denny.

"Hello."

"Hey, is this Kurt?"

"Yes, it is."

"Hey, Kurt, this is Denny Harris . . . sorry about that, I must have hit a dead spot."

"Not a problem," Kurt said. He looked at Sandy and nodded his head affirmatively, signifying to her that it was Denny who called back.

"Well, Randy Whitcomb gave me your number. He shared with me your story . . . Wow, what an experience. How are your wounds healing?"

"Very well, thank you for asking."

"So, what exactly happened?" Denny asked.

Kurt activated his speakerphone and spent the next ten minutes sharing the night he was shot. By now he had read the police report, talked with Jim Coleman, his partner, and with Mike Shell.

Denny informed Kurt he was coming to Chicago in a week, and he wanted to personally invite them to join him and Randy for dinner after one of the meetings. He wanted to hear more about his allegorical vision. Kurt agreed, thanked Denny, and told him he was looking forward to it. Kurt was flabbergasted and overwhelmed. He couldn't believe he was talking to a multi-millionaire.

Denny asked a few questions pertaining to Kurt's allegorical story, similar to the ones that Randy had asked. Kurt assured him that as far as he knew all the events were fictional. However, some of the things in his dream were factual, like the books and the particulars to certain procedures for network marketing. It just didn't add up. Kurt had little to no success in his actual MLM business before the vision; however, the information contained in his journey was profound and some of the teachings, he repeated, Kurt had not been exposed to before . . . and were principals that only high-level or top producers would be acquainted with.

Then Denny proceeded to encourage Kurt to work hard and, if he had to go back to the police force temporarily, he was not to consider it a setback, but a stepping-stone. It wasn't what Kurt wanted to hear, but because it was coming from Randy's mentor, it was easier to swallow.

Just when he thought he was relaxing, Denny told Kurt that he had a good feeling about him. He said that every now and again, there is a diamond in the rough.

"The opportunity to succeed in an MLM business is available to anyone, but not everyone chases the dream," Denny told Kurt. "I try not to make predictions about who I think will become the next millionaire, because there are so many variables. Even though I am only 34 years old, I have an eye for spotting underdogs who can become overcomers. After all, I've met a lot of people in this business.

"When Randy told me about you . . . what you've been through and this extraordinary illusion or whatever you call it . . . something jumped out at me. The first thing I thought of was a book or a movie. And the second thing was, *I must meet this man.* What I'm trying to say, Kurt, is that I talked to Randy and he agreed . . . I would like to be your mentor. What do you say?"

"I don't know what to say," Kurt said.

Sandy started to cry.

"Say 'yes.'"

SIXTEEN

The Limo Life

Sandy was in the kitchen unloading the bags of groceries, when Kurt came shuffling in. He never complained, but it was difficult for him to do much besides slowly walk from one room to another with one arm in a sling and a cane in the other, hobbling along with a limp.

"Let me help you with that," Kurt insisted even though he couldn't put anything away.

"Thanks hon, but why don't you take a seat and you can help me with something in a sec," Sandy said.

Kurt sat down at the kitchen table. He took a few items out of the bags and neatly organized them for easy access. He watched Sandy place the food in the freezer. When she shut the door and went to the pantry, Kurt stared at the pictures on the refrigerator. What pictures they did have — a car, a house, Disneyland, and others — were on one side. The idea was, when they reached a milestone, they would move the appropriate picture from the cooler side to the freezer side.

"You know what babe," Kurt said, "I think it's time we update our vision board and get new pictures on the fridge."

"Sounds great," Sandy replied.

"I want to get specific . . . I mean, let's start with small things, things we can accomplish sooner, to build a pattern of success. And, each time we reach that target, we celebrate it somehow, you know, with the kids. In fact, we should have Bryan and Lorrie put some pictures up there for them too," Kurt instructed.

Sandy stopped and said, "Kurt, that's an awesome idea."

"Thanks babe. I want to include the kids and let them share in the vision, the dream, and in the reward. But also, I want to find ways we can show our gratitude to those who join our team."

"One step ahead of ya," Sandy replied.

She picked up a plastic bag off the counter and placed it on the kitchen table in front of Kurt. "Take a look and tell me what you think," she said.

Kurt opened the bag and pulled out dozens of "Thank You" cards in packs of ten. Each pack had different shades of color on the envelopes and a variety of fancy writing and fonts. Immediately, Kurt figured out what Sandy was thinking . . . *Thank you cards, brilliant*, he thought.

"Tell me what you think of these," Sandy said as she handed him another bag.

He reached in and retrieved two massive plastic bags. He could not see what was inside because the bag was not transparent.

"I had an idea based on your comments concerning the Mercedes Benz," Sandy said.

Kurt opened the first bag, "No way," he said. He opened the second bag.

"The pink ones are for women and the black ones are for men," Sandy indicated by the color schemes to coincide with a gender theme.

Sandy had ordered two hundred key chains, one hundred for each gender. The key chains had a Mercedes Benz emblem.

"Turn it over," Sandy said.

Kurt turned over the key chain. Engraved on the backside was, "Believe the Dream."

"I thought we could give each person who joins the business and our team a key chain as a visual aid to inspire them to believe in their dream when they sign up. Is that alright?" Sandy asked.

"This is awesome, honey," Kurt said.

"I know," Sandy replied and then started giggling.

"I love it . . . simply love it," Kurt replied.

The two of them sat at the kitchen table signing their names to Thank You cards in preparation for future business. They had already had two meetings at their house. Randy gave the presentations. The first meeting, seven people showed up. The second meeting, there were 13 people. Sandy made appetizers for each meeting. Everyone was positive, and Randy modeled a perfect presentation.

After the second meeting was over, three of the prospects remained and talked further with Randy. All three joined the business that night! Sandy and Kurt were so excited. Randy commended them for their efforts and then discussed their strategy for working with the three new prospects.

It was Saturday, and Sandy and Kurt were getting ready for the MLM meeting. Denny Harris was speaking that evening at the Double Tree on 127th Street in Alsip. Kurt was a little anxious because he couldn't fit into pants yet. His leg bandage and brace were too large. He had been wearing shorts around the house and XXXL sweat pants when he left the house to go to the doctor.

Sandy went to the sporting goods store and purchased Kurt a couple of pairs of Nike stretch woven sweat pants. They had a dressier look and not so causal. It was a daily routine, but not a simple task to put on sweat pants. For Sandy, it was another positive sign demonstrating Kurt's willingness and passion to go out of his way to build the business.

Sandy also purchased a new sling with an immobilizer strap that wrapped around Kurt's back, which would make him more comfortable when he walked.

"Ready?" Sandy asked.

"Take a look at me; there's not much else you can do to make me any more ready," Kurt answered with a chuckle under his breath.

They entered the hotel. The lobby was huge with a large chandelier hanging from the twenty-foot ceiling and wrapped with marble walls and floors. They went to the table, signed in and received name tags.

The meeting hall had chairs lined in rows of twenty on each side and a seating capacity of 1,500 people. Naturally, they arrived early and found seats in the third row. They saved three seats for their new members of the network team.

It didn't take long for the room to fill. The noise of voices could be heard down the hall. Over a thousand people packed the room. Randy took the stage, greeted the crowd, and then introduced Denny.

Denny was charismatic, energetic, humorous, and inspiring. The atmosphere was electric and the information was compelling. He shared his testimony including his struggles and obstacles in the process of becoming a successful money earner in network marketing. Once he finished his story, he started in with his teaching.

"Okay, let me share with you some proven keys to becoming a successful networker." The large screen visualized his first point.

"Number One . . . you need to develop your dreams, goals and objectives. Studies conducted show that very few people have written out their dreams and goals. But those who achieve high levels of success do write out their dreams. What are your dreams? If time and money weren't inhibitors, what would your life be like? Be detailed in your dreams. Get mental images of your dream whether it be cars, homes, vacations, clothing, lifestyle, or whatever.

"It starts with your dreams and goals. Remember, a dream is the big picture, and goals are the steps that will get you to your dreams. For example, let's say your dream car is a Mercedes SL65 with a cost of $220,000 and a monthly payment of around $3,000. What are the steps you need to take to achieve that dream? An increase in your income might be necessary, so your goal would be to increase your monthly income to, $10,000 for example.

"You will have to break your goals down into bite-size objectives. For the example, this would be the things necessary to increase your monthly income to $10,000. Each day, you should review your dreams, goals and objectives in order to determine your daily activities. It doesn't hurt to get physical pictures and post these pictures in places around your home to be constant reminders of your dreams, goals and objectives."

Just then, Sandy looked at Kurt and smiled. They had just discussed the pictures on the refrigerator two days earlier, went to the store to purchase some magazines and also downloaded some photos from the Internet to enhance the vision board posted on the refrigerator.

Denny continued, "Number Two . . . you need to find a mentor."

This time, Kurt looked at Sandy and silently mouthed the word, WOW.

"This is probably the fastest way to build value and become an attractive leader," Denny said as he walked across the front of the platform. "I can't emphasize how crucial this is to building a massive downline. One of the most overlooked keys to success is to find someone who is already having the same kind of results that you want. It's important that you pick a mentor that will guide you and has leadership qualities that you can mirror and take on.

"Have you ever noticed that when you're around someone long enough, you soon start to act like them?"

The crowd reacted with laughter.

"I mean . . . really, you talk like them, you think like them. Well this is true regardless of whether a person is a negative or a positive person. Everything flows from the top down, and you will need success above you if you want it to flow down into the rest of you.

"So ask yourself, who are you hanging out with now? Successful leaders? Or people who are struggling and thinking negatively? Find a mentor or two that you can learn from, and do everything you can to be around them. Broke people can't help you get rich. Trust me.

"Number Three . . . sell yourself first. People are constantly presented with business opportunities every day, and you're going to have a difficult time separating yourself from the competition. It can be an unbearable uphill battle to sell your opportunity.

"The best way to overcome this hurdle is to sell yourself first. Be a leader that your prospects are drawn to because your confidence goes ahead of you before you ever mention your business opportunity and products. Gain their trust by teaching them how to build a business before asking for anything in return. Show them information, solutions, and a system they can use to be successful. By doing this, you sell yourself as a reliable and informed mentor that people will want to work with. As human beings, we're naturally attracted to leaders.

"Now, you may be saying, 'Denny, How do I educate and give valuable information to others when I'm not that successful?' If you thought that, I'm glad you did. The answer lies in the next key. . .

"Number Four . . . continue to learn. The network marketing industry is always evolving and always changing. It's continuously growing, and so should you. Stay current by reading newsletters, articles, by taking courses and attending seminars like this one.

"If you're new to the industry, then your objective at this point should be education! A vast majority of your time and effort should be focused upon learning. If you've been in network marketing for a while, then always be increasing your value. You don't want to get left behind.

"Let me ask you, when was the last time you purchased a marketing book and really studied it? Once you stop learning, you stop growing. Once you stop growing, so does your income!

"Number Five . . . don't give up too quickly. It's so easy to get discouraged early and get off track. You hear all the hype about people making six figures within their first month of business. Well to be honest with you, it doesn't happen that way. Unfortunately, many people in this industry hang all of their hopes on that hype, and bounce around from one business to another looking for the next big breakthrough.

"Have you heard the expression, 'grass is greener on the other side'"?

The audience responded, "Yeah."

"The truth is, it is greenest over a septic tank," Denny said.

The crowd broke out with a loud roar of laughter.

"And if you didn't get that because you city folk don't know what a septic tank is, ask somebody later to tell you. I'm originally from Dawson, Georgia, and that's all we had was a septic tank, there was no such thing as city plumbing."

Everyone laughed again. Kurt overhead a person in front of him say, "This guy is hilarious."

"Sooner or later, people need to realize that it's not the business or the product that's failing. It is themselves. The network marketing industry suffers from an alarming downline attrition rate, which means most people who join a business leave it within the first few months! Understand that network marketing success is like learning to play the piano. It rarely, if ever, happens overnight, and it takes a lot of practice. Sure, you can make a lot of money within your first year if you do things right, but you have to take small and measurable steps first.

"Dedicate yourself to grow your business every single day, even if it means spending just thirty minutes on it. Study, listen, read, participate in conference calls, and prospect on the phone."

Denny summarized his five points in closing and then talked about some of the products he had brought that night. There was a table at the back of the room with books, CDs and DVDs. After the meeting closed, Sandy and Kurt went straight to the product table to purchase his books and some CDs.

When they went to pay for the products, an older man in a dark blue suit came up beside Kurt and Sandy. Kurt noticed him out of his peripheral vision, but he didn't turn to see what he wanted. Then, the man tapped Kurt on the shoulder and said, "Are you Kurt Dungy?"

"Yes," Kurt replied.

"And you must be Sandy," he said.

Kurt took notice of how the leaders in his organization remembered their names when they spoke to him and Sandy. He remembered reading the importance of using names when he read, *How to Win Friends and Influence People.*

"My name is Bernie."

Sandy and Kurt greeted him with a handshake. Bernie had white hair, but he looked young in face and in good physical shape. Bernie had been in network marketing for twenty years and was a servant. Kurt would get to know Bernie. His reputation was impeccable and he was at every convention and meeting. He assisted Randy in the organization of each meeting, and he was the first person Randy signed up in his business.

"If you will follow me, please, I will show you where you need to go," Bernie said.

Kurt assumed he was referring to meeting up with Randy and Denny, so they went along like it was planned. Bernie directed them out of the meeting hall, down the hallway and into an office suite near the front lobby.

When they walked in, there were already about twenty people in the room. Three people were dressed in black, with a vest and bow tie, pouring beverages and carrying a fruit tray, offering drinks and fruit to the people gathered. Randy saw Kurt and Sandy and waived, signaling for them to approach.

The crowd remained for about thirty to forty minutes and then disbanded. Randy instructed Kurt and Sandy to ride with him and Denny. When they exited the lobby, a stretch limousine was parked at the entrance. They entered.

Inside were several other people who Kurt and Sandy didn't know. They felt a little awkward at first. Once Kurt sat down, he thought how different it was to be seated in the back of a limo. He envisioned again, the man who held the door assisting Sandy into the back of the limo and then he envisioned himself opening the car door of his patrol car, assisting a criminal into the back of his cruiser. He laughed inside.

"What's so funny," Sandy asked.

Still chuckling to himself, Kurt answered, "I'll tell you later."

They reached their destination and exited the vehicle. Everyone paraded inside the lobby. They were at the Melting Pot of Chicago, a fine dining restaurant. After being seated, the waiter came, gave the specials, and then distributed menus.

Kurt opened his menu and looked at the Fondue Fusion and below the entrees was the price, $92 per couple. *Good God, Almighty,* Kurt said to himself and then looked at Sandy, bringing to her attention the price of a meal.

Just then, Denny spoke out, "Everyone! Dinner is on me tonight so order whatever you want."

Kurt felt a bit embarrassed, hoping that his facial reaction didn't cause Denny to say what he just said at that moment.

Randy introduced the group to everyone, giving a brief overview of the time and success in the business, and then he introduced Kurt and Sandy.

"And, one of the newest members of my downline, Kurt and Sandy Dungy . . . and in case you're wondering . . . Kurt is one of Chicago's finest and . . . how long ago?" Randy asked Kurt.

"Five weeks," Kurt answered.

"Five weeks ago, Kurt was responding to a robbery in progress and was shot," Randy said.

Everyone gasped at one time, some of the guests said things like, "Seriously. . . Oh my gosh, and . . . Wow."

"Initially, Kurt was with me about two years ago. He went through some challenges, but now he's back."

The group responded immediately with applause and cheers.

"That's right, he's back!" Randy said enthusiastically.

Everyone continued to celebrate Kurt and Sandy's restart in the business.

"Take a few minutes, Kurt, and tell us what happened," Randy said.

Kurt shared a modified version of his incident . . . the night he was shot, and Sandy told her side of the story. They didn't mention anything about Kurt's vision while under his induced coma. They just stuck to the traumatic event and the recovery process.

"How soon before you're able to return to the force?" Bernie asked.

"A few more months . . . maybe four or five, I guess, depending on my leg. They're not sure how long it will take and it's too soon to know if I can pass the physical exam to be out on duty," Kurt responded reluctantly. He had already made it clear to Randy that his goal was not to return to his job, with high hopes his business would grow enough to sustain them. In addition, Kurt remembered what Denny said about not feeling frustrated if he did have to go back to work for a season, so he answered Bernie's question accordingly.

They spent the evening sharing stories, bragging on those who were doing well and achieving their goals. Kurt observed that no one spoke negatively about anyone who was struggling or falling behind in their downline. In fact, they referred to the ones who were not producing as ones who were "overcoming obstacles to obtain their dream."

After dinner, Bernie gave Kurt and Sandy a ride back to the hotel, where their car was parked. Bernie chatted about his family and his relationship with Randy. Kurt and Sandy witnessed a group of people who were more than business associates. They were a family. That night was an example as to how the business develops relationships and cultivates long-term friendships.

SEVENTEEN

Girl Scout Cookies

Sandy was driving Kurt back from his checkup with Dr. McConnell; since he was a surgeon, he referred Kurt over to a physical therapist. In order to gain full mobility in his shoulder and his leg, Kurt was going to need exercise. His early calisthenics would include some basic workouts, beginning with a five pound hand weight and short daily walks.

On the ride home, Kurt referred back to the allegorical vision and its irony to his current circumstances. He sat quietly, pondering the scenario and wondered how, in any way, was his dream tied to his present situation.

"You're quiet," Sandy said.

Kurt remained silent.

Sandy looked at Kurt and said, "Are you alright?"

"I'll be fine."

"Anything you want to talk about?" Sandy asked.

She gave him a few moments, thinking he was gathering his thoughts. But after a long silence, she decided to pry. "What's wrong, Kurt . . . you worried about getting better?"

"Nah," he mumbled.

"Then, what is it?"

"Why is this happening to me?"

That made Sandy nervous. She immediately lifted her foot off the gas pedal and slowed the car down.

"Alright Kurt, you're scaring me . . . what's going on?"

"I don't know. It's probably nothing. I'm trying to figure out why I had that vision and what does it mean. Is it supposed to mean anything? Is it a sign . . . a sign from God, or something? Think about it, Sandy. In my vision, my doctor referred me to a therapist."

"Go on," she said.

"From what I can gather, and the comments from Denny and Randy, the doctor represented my direct upline and the therapist represented my mentor.

"What are the odds that my upline would be Randy Whitcomb? Man, he's the top earner in all of Chicago and coincidently, his upline is Denny Harris . . . who just happens to be the richest person in our company. Don't you see the paradox?"

"Kinda," Sandy replied. She really didn't at the moment, but she wanted to be supportive. She was afraid to say "no" and have it cause Kurt to clam up and not discuss it with her.

"Why me?" Kurt asked.

"I don't know why . . . to be honest, Kurt. But what I do know is we have a chance to change the course of our lives. Our kids can have a future. For some reason, this happened to make a difference."

"You're probably right," Kurt reluctantly agreed.

"You haven't mentioned this in a long time, so I haven't brought it up until now. But when we first joined the business a couple of years ago, it was just six months after your father died. One night after a meeting, we were driving home and . . . out of nowhere, you said, 'One of the things we're going to do is donate money to the American Cancer Society.' Do you remember that?" Sandy asked.

A light bulb went off in Kurt's mind. His memory raced back to that moment when he said those words. "I totally forgot about that," he said.

"Kurt, you joined the police force because you wanted to help people. That's who you are . . . you're a giver. But over the years, the job hardened you. Maybe it was because you were always dealing with criminals, murderers, and people who preyed on the weak.

"Since your injury and the three day vision, you've changed. The Kurt I met years ago is back, the one who always gave in and bought ten boxes of Girl Scout cookies because he couldn't say "no" to those little girls, who in your words, had an entrepreneur spirit."

Kurt laughed. "I always did buy too many cookies, didn't I?"

"It's not that," Sandy said. "It's what you did with them. You took every one of the boxes and gave them away to total strangers; people you would meet while on patrol. You never ate one. You gave them away.

"This business may not be for everyone. But for us, it is. Yes, it's hard. Yes, we have to put a lot of effort into it. Yes, we sacrifice our time, energy and all we do is eat and sleep network marketing. But for us, it's our ticket to do what we love to do best, and that's to help others . . . people who are less fortunate and are hurting.

"Sure, the money will be rewarding. But the real reward will come when we do what you did with the Girl Scout cookies. But I think it's bigger than that. There are millions of people out there, going to work every day, slaving to get ahead. They work forty to sixty hours a week and at the end of the year, they are not much farther ahead than the year before, even if they were fortunate enough to get a raise.

"But they're out there working to make money for someone else. They work for money instead of money working for them.

"Kurt, I've always believed that you'd become something great. I look at you and see how you've overcome so much. You chose to drop out of high school before the eleventh grade and went to work to help support your family after your mom got sick. Then, a few years later, you joined the academy and became a police officer. In a few short years, you were a homicide detective, then a SWAT operative with Special Forces and the drug task force.

"You've excelled at everything, and now it's your time."

Kurt turned and looked at Sandy. *What an amazing woman*, he thought.

"Kurt, I would rather work hard for the next four years and begin to watch the business pay for itself, than work the next forty years and wonder what life would have been like if we hadn't started in the business.

"Sure, Randy and Denny might be right . . . your story could do well. But I believe it's more than a book. It's a blessing. We can give hope to others who didn't have a vision, or get shot on the job. But you did. And ya know what, we have a choice. To use it for good or lose the significance of it. . . Giving out Girl Scout cookies."

Kurt laughed again.

"Girl Scout cookies," he said.

"Think of it. We've been afforded the opportunity to do something good . . . No, something great! Our business offers some great products, products we're proud of. But the system we possess! A system that shows how to own your business and become an entrepreneur is what this nation was founded upon."

When Sandy said that, Kurt remembered in his vision when they were riding home from Dr. Kay's office and Sandy played a CD from a woman in an MLM business that said the same exact thing. *Déjà vu*, Kurt said in his mind.

"We have the Girl Scout cookies . . . the business model that can bring financial freedom and help people achieve their dreams. That's why it's happened to you, Kurt. Because we are going do something significant if we keep doing what we're doing."

"Giving away Girl Scout cookies," Kurt said . . . then started laughing.

"Giving away Girl Scout cookies," Sandy repeated in agreement, and then laughed along with him.

"You know, you're on to something there," Kurt said. "Those girls came to our house every year. And once I bought a box from one girl, another one would show up the next day. And then, another, and another and another. They spread the word to their girlfriends that they knew a guy who would buy their cookies if they just asked a simple question, 'Would you like to buy some Girl Scout cookies'?"

"It was that simple, 'Would you like to buy some Girl Scout cookies?' It was nothing difficult or pushy, just a simple question. I mean, think of it Sandy. What those girls were basically saying was, 'Can you help me'?

"It's a simple question! Can you help me? That's what people are looking for . . . help. And my answer is, 'Yes I can.' Every person out there is looking for a job, or is working at one that is not able to pay their bills or send their kids to college, let alone get ahead. People are struggling for hope, and we have the answer.

"It's that simple. Prospecting is simply that, offering help. That's probably the most important question we could ask in network marketing, 'How can I help you?'

"That's why this is happening to me," Kurt said. "If we really believe the system and see it as "the" method for obtaining financial freedom and achieving a dream, then we just need to ask those who don't know what we know, 'how can I help you'?"

"That's tight," Sandy said.

"What?" Kurt said in shock with Sandy's choice of words.

"That's what Bryan says," Sandy replied. "I think it means, 'that's a great idea,' or what you just said was profound . . . tight."

"I know what it means," Kurt responded. "I just didn't expect that from you."

"I'm hip," Sandy said.

"They don't say that anymore, hon. It's . . . I'm straight," Kurt said. They both started laughing. Once they started, they couldn't stop. They just kept on, until Kurt was holding his stomach. Sandy was giggling so hard, she was crying.

Just when he started to get control of his impulsive giggling spell, Kurt looked at Sandy, and her mascara was running down her face. He pointed to her face and Sandy looked in the mirror.

"Oh, great," she said.

Kurt opened the glove box, retrieved some "left over" napkins from a takeout restaurant and handed one to Sandy. When she wiped her face, she smeared it all over her cheeks.

They stopped at a red light, and teenagers in the car in the next lane saw Kurt and Sandy laughing and her mascara running down her face. It made it even more hilarious, and they continued to cackle as they drove off.

The model of the Girl Scout cookies and the question, "How can I help you?" . . . became a motivation for Kurt and Sandy. It no longer seemed like work, but a way to help others. Kurt found a picture of his dad and put it up on the refrigerator as a reminder. Someday, he would write a large donation to the American Cancer Society. He found his purpose through Girl Scout cookies.

Weeks turned into months, and Kurt and Sandy worked the business diligently. They averaged two to three meetings a week and added close to eight new members every week. The growth was unusual and remarkable.

In their first six months, they personally recruited 179 people and obtained an additional 213 persons in their downline. They could no longer fit in their house, so they started renting the local fire hall in their township. The fire chief was a friend of Kurt's, and he helped them get a great deal.

Their checks were pouring in every week now, and by their sixth month, Kurt and Sandy were bringing in about $2,700 a month. Their growth spurt was extraordinary, but they were fortunate enough to continue to receive a paycheck with Kurt's job, which enabled them to work full-time in the business. In fact, they worked nearly sixty-five to eighty hours a week.

It came time . . . time for Kurt to return to his precinct. His leg injury was only ninety percent, so he was assigned a desk job. Denny stayed in regular contact, and about this time, he called Kurt to encourage him to go back to work and wait until he had a larger payout and a consistent stream of income before he quit his job.

EIGHTEEN

The Plateau

It was Kurt's first day back to work. He was bent over tying his shoes when Sandy came into the bedroom. He sat up and saw her. She stood in the doorway and smiled. It had been a while since she had seen him in his blues. He stood up and grabbed his tie, walked to the mirror on Sandy's dresser to clip it on his shirt. Sandy then walked behind him, peeked around his shoulder and then saluted him. He grinned at her gesture.

"This soon shall pass," she said in reference to his return.

"Not soon enough," he replied.

"At least it's not the graveyard shift," she said.

"That's true," Kurt responded.

Kurt turned around and put his arms around Sandy. She looked straight up into his eyes. He leaned down and gave her a kiss.

"Where would I be without you?" he said.

"Broke and depressed," she piped back.

They laughed.

Kurt just held her and stared. He was more frustrated about not being able to be home and work the business than he was about going back to work. He and Sandy had a routine, a system that they worked together. Their goal was to continue hosting meetings at the fire hall, but he wasn't sure about getting days off to make the out-of-town trips.

"Now, don't you worry about a thing; I will keep the calendar updated and continue to input the progress in the Excel report so we know where we are. All the Thank You cards are signed and I ordered another shipment of Mercedes key chains," Sandy said.

"You're awesome," he replied and then kissed her. Before she had a chance to reply, Kurt quickly replied, "I know!"

Sandy laughed and Kurt grinned. Their brief exchange before his departure that morning made things better and lifted his spirit.

Kurt made it through his first day, mostly filling out reports and becoming familiar with a computer. Fortunately, the time he spent with Sandy over the past few months exposed him to software that he'd normally not use. He wasn't computer illiterate; he had used one in his patrol car. However, this was a different program, and it was going to take some time to adjust.

Two months went by, and Kurt was doing a good job, but his heart wasn't in policing anymore. During his lunch break, he would go outside, make his calls, and send texts to his downline and prospects. Sandy took over the business. She never complained, but it was difficult doing it alone. Kurt decided it was best to cut back to one meeting a week. It seemed like a good idea at the time, but having two meetings a week for the past eight months caused people to get into a pattern, while some had schedule conflicts once the change was made. So it affected the attendance more than what they thought it would.

After Kurt made the decision, Randy called him the next day saying that he wished he had known ahead of time before they made the decision, he would have been willing to host it for Kurt. This was unlike Kurt, because up until now, he had run everything by Randy. Kurt quickly apologized for making the decision without informing Randy in advance. There wasn't much they could do about it right then. The fire department already rented the hall out for that day. They were either going to need to find another location or wait six months for the lease to expire.

Over the next few weeks, Kurt slowed down making calls during his lunch break. Sandy picked up the slack, but she found herself juggling her schedule with the kids. She recommended that they hire someone to come in and clean the house so she could focus on the business more, but Kurt objected saying that he didn't want to lose the money.

Sandy was busy running Lorrie to cheerleading practice. Bryan joined the basketball team and was taking guitar lessons as well. The evenings were filled with making calls to prospects, the once-a-week conference call, a meeting at the fire hall and balancing Bryan's game schedule two nights a week.

Bryan's grades started to suffer, and his coach warned him that he had to maintain at least a "B" GPA in order to stay on the team. Lorrie had afternoon games, and Bryan's were in the evening. The evenings were beginning to overwhelm Sandy, and Kurt wasn't able to attend all the functions.

The business remained steady but was not growing at the pace it was previously. Kurt started to get frustrated and was hoping that he would be able to quit his job after six months, but at the rate they were going, that didn't look likely. Working two jobs wasn't easy for Kurt, and he was having a hard time keeping up with his downline. He was missing calls and didn't have the time to follow up with everyone like he had in the past.

They were adding people every week, but due to his schedule and Sandy running the kids everywhere, they were losing as many as they were putting into the business every month. Kurt was getting frustrated and Sandy was getting tired.

In the meantime, Sandy and Kurt had made a commitment to Denny that they would write out their story, and Denny was willing to pay for the printing with hopes of it becoming a bestseller. But after three months, they stopped working on the manuscript. Kurt's health still wasn't 100 percent, and he had to exercise daily in order to get his leg back in shape.

Ten months had passed since the shooting, and Kurt had to appear before the district attorney's office for his preliminary deposition. Even though the appallete court was prosecuting the inmates who were involved in the robbery and shooting of Kurt, motions and appeals were going to delay a trial for another year or more.

Every day, Kurt dreaded going to work. He wanted to quit his job, but the business was stagnating. For every two persons Kurt and Sandy put in their downline, they would lose one. It began to take a toll on Kurt. He wanted to quit his job and just couldn't seem to get over the hump.

Meanwhile, Bryan's grades continued to decline and he was no longer eligible to play sports. Bryan was frustrated because he didn't feel that his mother or father cared about him because they didn't want to pay for the tutoring. They felt Bryan should study harder, so when he was removed from the basketball team, it happened a week before the district playoffs. Bryan blamed his parents, and it made him become bitter.

Of course, this affected more than just Bryan. Kurt felt that he had let Bryan down and that Bryan would blame his father for being kicked off the basketball team. This scenario took its toll on Kurt more than it did on Bryan because Kurt feared that his vision would revisit his family. That fear gripped Kurt's heart and instead of working harder, he worried that his allegorical vision would come to pass.

The business was still maintaining and providing additional income, but that's not what Kurt wanted. He wanted it to grow so he could quit his job. Kurt's one-year anniversary for the shooting was approaching soon and he was frustrated because he wanted to leave his job no later than one year, and it didn't look like he would reach his goal.

Randy and Kurt remained in constant contact since Kurt returned to his job. Every two to three days, like clockwork, Randy would call and check in on Kurt.

The last few times Randy spoke with Kurt, he sensed that Kurt was getting tired. Kurt and Sandy had made such progress, but the pressures at home, Kurt's job, and Sandy's "yellow cab" service were taking too much time away from the business. She was behind in the data entering . . . something she had never allowed to happen before. Once Randy noticed a change in Kurt's tone on the phone, he knew it was time for a face-to-face meeting.

Randy and Kurt met at a local coffee shop. They had small talk at first and then Randy took over the conversation. He praised Kurt for his success and reminded him of where he'd come from and how much progress he had made in such a short time. At first, Kurt wasn't receptive to his praise because the goals he had set for himself had not fulfilled yet, and he didn't like it at all.

The first thing Randy did was revisit the dream. He continued to probe Kurt concerning his dreams, goals and aspirations.

"Kurt, after 23 years in this business, there is one thing I have never forgotten," Randy said.

"What's that?" Kurt inquired.

"Revisiting the dream," Randy replied. "Let me tell you something, Kurt; the dream inside is what keeps you alive! You have to revisit it in some way, everyday. You've heard it hundreds of times, but I will never stop quoting it, 'don't let your obstacles become bigger than your dreams.' Working two jobs isn't part of your dream, is it Kurt?"

"No."

"Then I want you to go back to what we did in the beginning, when you restarted in the company . . . do you remember?"

"Set bite-size goals," Kurt answered.

"Exactly! You know the drill," Randy reinforced. "Have a dream . . . set goals . . . make a strategy . . . put a plan into action . . . expect and analyze results," Kurt quoted the five steps for success in the MLM business. Don't beat yourself up, Kurt. You and Sandy have done a remarkable job!"

"If I could just quit my job . . . I'd be happier," Kurt said.

"I'm sure . . . but timing is everything," Randy replied.

"It seems like I just don't have enough of it," Kurt responded.

"Enough of what?" Randy asked.

"Time," Kurt answered.

"Kurt, I've been right where you are."

"You have?"

"Yes, and I know what is like to taste success and then have it plateau. It is common with anyone who works hard at this."

"What do I do?"

"Manage your time."

"That's just it, I don't have enough time."

"We all have 168 hours in a week," Randy said. "It's the same for everyone. It's not the amount of time, but what we do with the time we have."

"Any suggestions?" Kurt asked.

"Yes, I want you to spend equal time with me and your mentor, Denny, and then select two people from your downline and reciprocate knowledge. We can get so busy at doing the work we forget that it's based upon relationships. It's a simple procedure. Hang around people who make exceptionally more than what you make. Denny is always available, and you need to spend time on the phone with him and me more than you do with prospects."

"Really?"

"Yes, especially at times like these. Face it, you reached a plateau and you will come out of it if you stay close to us. You're of no value if you can't still be filled. Every leader needs to be filled. We are always giving and if you don't refill, you'll burn out and then be of no value to your downline.

"There's a major conference coming up next month in Phoenix called Network Marketing Mastermind Event. I want you to attend it. Do whatever it takes, but you need to be there. I want you to go early with me so we can spend two days with Denny before the conference begins. Let's make it happen."

NINETEEN

Fly with the Eagles

It was time to take charge of the situation. Kurt and Sandy sat down with Bryan and Lorrie. They helped set goals for both of them and a system of rewards for their academic success and behavioral achievements. All four sat around the kitchen table discussing their dreams. For Bryan it was a BMW Roadster and for Lorrie, it was veterinarian school. Sandy had the laptop and made each of them search for their dream item and price it. When Bryan saw how much a brand new car cost, he recommended he look at used cars. Kurt laughed and said, "Relax, son, were not getting you one anytime soon."

Sandy and Kurt chuckled a bit. Bryan didn't think it was so funny. "Then what's the sense of looking up a price?" he asked.

"First it's a dream and then a goal. Knowing how much it cost tells you what you need to believe for, and then you make a plan to get it," Kurt said.

"I've got a plan," Bryan said.

"And what's that?" Sandy asked.

"I pass the twelfth grade and then you surprise me by buying the car for a graduation gift . . . that's my plan!"

They laughed together.

"That's my plan, too," Lorrie added.

Sandy giggled and said, "I think we've gotta work on that plan a little."

Then Kurt said, "Honey, wanna show 'em now?"

"Show us what?" Lorrie asked.

"Is my Beemer in the garage?" Bryan replied. He got up from the table and started toward the garage entrance door off the kitchen.

"Come back here son, your car's not out there," Kurt said.

"What do you want to show us then?" Bryan asked.

Sandy slid the laptop over and on the screen was a large vacation cruise ship.

"No way!" Bryan exclaimed.

"We're buying a boat?" Lorrie asked.

"Wow, you're special," Bryan said.

"What?" Lorrie replied.

"It's a cruise ship for vacations," Bryan said.

"That's right," Sandy added. "We're going on a cruise to the Caribbean Islands . . . all of us."

"When?" Lorrie asked.

"Hopefully, this fall . . . after hurricane season," Kurt replied.

Sandy returned the conversation back to the kids and their dreams. They were instructed to find a picture that represented what they wanted and to place it on the refrigerator. It didn't matter what it was, Sandy and Kurt wanted to teach the principal of having a dream. It didn't matter what field of study or occupation they chose, they felt it was a positive reinforcement and a way to introduce the entrepreneur spirit inside of them.

~

Three weeks later, Kurt and Sandy were on their way to Houston for the Mastermind Event. Kurt saved his vacation time for the cruise, but he also had accumulated enough time to spend a few days in Texas. They were not only excited to go on the trip, but they were going to spend some quality time with Denny and Randy. Both of them supported Kurt and Sandy, and it wasn't just because of Kurt's special revelation. They were like that with everyone.

They modeled a system of building and cultivating relationships that was also Kurt and Sandy's method of building their team. In fact, after Randy met with Kurt and helped him through his plateau, Kurt and Sandy barbecued three weekends in a row, inviting all the members of their team from the Chicago area. They sent invitations to all members in every state. They were surprised that 56 people flew in for the celebration. They gave special gifts to the top earners, but everyone received a 5" x 7" photograph of a white Mercedes Benz in a picture frame for attending, as a token of appreciation.

They did it in response to the way their mentor taught them. Denny was always doing something to show his gratitude to those in his downline, just on a bigger scale. And, the barbecues paid dividends. In two weeks, their team brought in a record 72 new members. And the week of their trip to Phoenix an additional 23 people joined their team.

Kurt followed Randy's advice. He was spending the core of his time with his top earners and in phone calls with Denny and Randy. It was like a rocket taking off at NASA. The burden of growing the business was lifted as they cultivated relationships and rewarded people with endorsements.

Kurt and Sandy were very close to becoming Diamonds, and their monthly income was vastly approaching $4,500. Denny and Randy bragged on Kurt and Sandy to everyone. In just ten months, they were the fastest growing team in the organization.

Kurt's coworkers in his precinct knew he was in an MLM business, but they had no idea he was earning as much in his part-time job as he was as a police officer. At first, upon Kurt's return to the job, he was the brunt of several practical jokes and the rumor mill for his involvement in network marketing, but over time, people couldn't help respect him for his friendly attitude and sense of pleasant personality. A few of the police officers eventually joined Kurt's downline. One of them was Mike

Shell. Mike spent every chance he could to build his business and Kurt helped him grow.

Kurt and Sandy felt like a king and queen. They had the VIP package and a limo picked them up from their hotel and took them to the coliseum. The anticipation and excitement was contagious with nearly 15,000 people registered for the life-changing event. The host was the richest person in MLM, and the "Rock Star" presenters were the top money earners from a variety of MLM organizations. In addition, there were more than 150 leaders in attendance that made approximately a million dollars annually. Sandy and Kurt viewed the schedule in advance, but couldn't decide which session to attend.

They met with Denny and Randy the night before and they guided them to which seminars to select and gave backgrounds on each of the keynote speakers. One of the lecturers was Julia McDaniel whose background was so similar to one of the characters in Kurt's vision. When Denny started to tell her story, Kurt finished it with precision.

"Oh, you've heard of her . . . that's great," Denny said.

"No, I haven't," Kurt replied.

"Did Randy give you one of her CDs?" Denny inquired further.

"She is one of the characters from Kurt's vision," Sandy said.

"She is?" Denny replied.

"Well not her . . . the woman in my dream had a different name, but her story is nearly identical," Kurt said.

Denny looked at Randy and grinned. Both Denny and Randy had listened to the story, but only once, so there was no way they could be as familiar as Kurt and Sandy were, especially because they hadn't finished writing the storyline into a manuscript.

"She's the woman that we . . . in the dream . . . were listening to in Las Vegas when Kurt fell asleep on the front row," Sandy added.

They were briefly sidetracked from the conference and talked about Kurt's vision. Denny asked when he could see a copy.

"We can email it to you if you'd like," Sandy said. "We have a copy on our laptop."

"With you?" Denny asked.

"With us," Kurt answered.

Denny was one of the "Rock Star" presenters, so he was able to reserve seats for Kurt, Sandy, Randy and Melissa (Randy's wife), and a few other associates from Denny's team.

"Isn't she going to be at your conference later this year?" Randy asked Denny. He was referring to Julia who paralleled to the female character in Kurt's dream.

"In fact, she is . . . you guys need to come to that," Denny insisted. "It's in Phoenix . . . it will be off the chain."

"Oh, I don't. . ." Kurt stammered to say.

"We are planning a vacation with our kids, what are the dates?" Sandy asked.

"Don't worry about it now. Let's enjoy this one, and we'll work something out," Randy interjected.

Randy and Denny already knew that Kurt and Sandy were very close to becoming a Diamond. The company was about to award them with a Mercedes, but Kurt's upline and mentor had decided to give them a free vacation to the Caribbean Islands for being the fastest growing team in the organization, but they were keeping it a secret to surprise them. So, the invitation to the conference in Phoenix was a setup.

Kurt and Sandy were excited and especially interested to listen to Julia. They could hardly contain themselves. They found their seat and waited for the main event to begin.

"Whatever you do, don't fall asleep on me," Sandy said.

Kurt quickly turned and looked at her. Sandy busted out laughing, "I'm just kidding," she said.

"Very funny," Kurt said as he shook his head in response to her sarcasm and choice of humor. Sandy always knew how to make Kurt smile, even at the oddest times.

Steve Piston, the event host, greeted the crowd.

Everyone stood to their feet and cheered like they were at a rock concert.

"He looks like Dr. McCarty," Sandy said.

"Would you stop," Kurt replied while clapping his hands.

"Just saying . . . he matches your description," Sandy said.

Steve introduced Julia, and the crowd roared with thunderous applause.

"Thank you, Steve, for that wonderful introduction. It's such a delight to be here tonight and be back again at this wonderful conference.

"Is this first class or what people?"

Everyone stood again and cheered.

Julia shared her testimony . . . the highs and the lows, and then dove into a powerful teaching.

"I've been asked tonight to speak on the things I do when I start or restart someone into the business. I've taught this many times before, but once it comes down to it, everything we do, prospecting, making calls, showing presentations . . . of all the stuff we do, getting a person signed up and plugged in is what makes this industry so significant and how you work yourself out of a J-O-B.

"I want to share with you tonight ten things I would do to start or restart someone in my business and I hope it helps you in yours.

"First, it begins with a question, why do it? This needs to be settled as the foundation for being involved in network marketing. It is important to get a very clear reason on the 'why.' Why I am doing this business? Is it a pain to avoid, or a pleasure to gain? You need a compelling reason as to why you would choose this industry, because that answer is what will keep you in it.

"Second . . . Have a burning desire for exactly 'what' it is that you want to accomplish. No one can answer that but you. It has to come from within you. Your passion. Your dream. Your desires are yours and no one else's. When you define the 'what' no one can steal it from you. Develop a 'nothing's going to stop me' attitude.

"Third . . . Set your goals and get very specific with a business plan. Map out your activity . . . your income . . . your promotion dates for the next one month, three months, six months, and for the year. Then, here's the kicker . . . develop your ultimate goal that can be achieved in the next five years. That's right, write a five-year biography as if it has already happened. Include dates, the month, the season . . . tell what you believe you can achieve during that time frame.

"Fourth . . . Share your dream with those you love and are supportive, including your upline and your mentor, if it is someone besides your upline. Ask your mentor to coach you, make you accountable by giving them permission to speak into your life. Set up intervals of time for progress reports and ways to track your successes and setbacks.

"Fifth . . . Put your goals into action. Decide and determine your ROM, which stands for Reach Out Methods. In other words, start scheduling. Use a calendar and let it be your guide. Begin with a two-week strategy. Fill it with appointments and activities. Write down the books or CDs you want to devour. And be sure to overbook! Always keep your calendar full. Watch it closely and pour it on if it's looking bare.

"Sixth . . . Get organized. A carpenter or a mechanic who misplaces his tools cannot finish a job in a timely matter, and sometimes, not at all. Keep your tools in a set place.

"Do you need catalogs, sponsoring brochures, CDs, order forms? Whatever your organization uses to promote or educate, make sure you have plenty of them.

"If your reach out methods . . . ROM . . . are in a cold market, then handle the details before you get started.

"Have a day planner for your pipeline and follow up. Never underestimate the importance in the details. Go the extra mile, especially when it comes to reminder calls, thank you cards, pre-profiling and follow-up procedures. This way you can be efficient, organized and increase your potential. Give impeccable service.

"Seventh . . . Stay consistent. You can do your business part-time but not sometime. Focus on the basics and repeat the cycle. Here's a four step strategy . . . schedule, sell, sponsor, and follow-up.

"Eighth . . . Stay connected. Whatever night your training call falls on, it's important to participate. And, encourage your people to do the same. Utilize technology, be it texts or sending emails. It's important to have people's email addresses. This saves time and creates efficient follow through.

"Remember this, hot coals stay hotter when they're together."

The crowd laughed and then applauded.

"Are you learning anything?" Julia asked the audience. To which she received a unanimous, "YES!"

"Ninth . . . Duplicate the system. It is important that you stick with the system in your organization. The leaders in your company spend time and energy to develop a proven plan of action and you have to trust them.

"Teach those you've sponsored to do the same thing you're doing. Even if their goals are different than yours, they'll employ the same system for whatever level of success they so desire.

"Tenth, and finally . . . Enjoy the journey. The process goes in cycles and seasons. You'll never stop analyzing your goals, strategies or plan of action. In order to produce the results you want, you will have to revisit your steps to success.

"Ten things to start or restart . . . Why do it? Have a burning desire, set goals, share your dream, put your goals into actions, get organized, stay consistent, stay connected, duplicate the system, and number ten . . . enjoy the journey.

"Thank you," Julia said, and she went to her seat.

During the applause, Kurt got a text from Denny that read, "Do you want to meet Julia?"

TWENTY

The Mercedes Milestone

After the main session was over, Denny texted Randy to meet him back at the hotel lobby. Denny rented a car for the week, but Randy, Melissa, Kurt and Sandy rode in the limousine back to the hotel. They rendezvoused in the lobby near the waterfall. Denny pulled up in a black Cadillac Escalade. This luxurious SUV came with a third row, plenty of leg and headroom and was visually impressive . . . something Denny would drive.

To an outsider, Denny appeared flashy, but he was a very humble and giving man. He, like many other MLM leaders, supported orphanages, foundations, and provided leadership roles in humanitarian efforts around the world.

Being his usual energetic self . . . Denny jumped out, opened the back door on the driver's side, ran over to the other side, opened the other back door, and then reached in and moved the seats to make the third row accessible. Kurt and Sandy entered the third row. Randy and

Melissa climbed in the middle row and Denny, with his wife, Lisa, were up front.

They arrived at the restaurant, the Fogo de Chão at the Galleria. It was Brazilian steakhouse cuisine. There were six other people besides Denny's party, and a large table was prepared in a back room. The guests were the "who's who" in MLM and Julia McDaniel was one of them.

Before they walked back to be seated, Denny pulled Kurt and Sandy aside to tell them not to mention the vision experience, to wait until another time. Denny wanted to read it first and protect Kurt and the content of the storyline.

"Just be yourself," Denny instructed Kurt and Sandy. "Enjoy the journey," he quoted from Julia's point number ten, then smiled and laughed. It broke the ice and made them feel relaxed. They took a deep breath and followed Randy and Denny to the back area.

Introductions were made and everyone found a seat around the table. The food was unbelievable, the conversation was simple and fun hearted. It amazed Kurt and Sandy how normal and ordinary the top money earners were. They didn't carry themselves like they were something special or important. They were just the opposite — friendly, kind and courteous.

Julia asked about Sandy's children. She quickly memorized Bryan and Lorrie's name and used them when she inquired into their lives. Julia acted interested, as if Bryan and Lorrie were her grandchildren. They exchanged family photos from their cell phones and talked about raising kids.

It was a night to remember and Kurt and Sandy were so thrilled, when they got back to the hotel they couldn't sleep. So, instead, they sat on the balcony of their room and talked until three in the morning. Something was becoming very clear to them — success was more than money; it's about building relationships, helping others, extending and receiving love to others and giving.

~

Over the next two months, Kurt and Sandy were seeing incredible results. They took advantage of the material and information they obtained at the Mastermind Event and taught it to their team. Kurt's team was repeating everything he taught his leaders and the energy was more than emotion, it was results.

Each week they added over 70 people to their downline. The leaders were spending 15 to 29 hours a week working the business, prospecting, showing the plan, making calls, participating in the training calls and attending the monthly team meeting.

The fire hall was too small now. It could only seat 350 people, and now they were having over 500 people in attendance. Kurt invested in a camera, audio and computer equipment, and his monthly meetings were streamed live via the internet. Now all his team could view the meetings. Kurt wanted the technology in place to afford online viewers to ask questions or give their testimony in a live setting. The buzz was hitting the organization and everyone knew about Kurt's team. It even had a nickname, The Cop Shop. Kurt didn't like it at first, but over time, it stuck and he didn't object. He never called it that, but that was how people remembered his group. He was the cop who was shot and a business was born.

Sandy and Julia hit it off in Houston. They stayed in touch regularly, texting each other nearly every day. Julia's organization was involved in orphanages in third world countries. Sandy told the story about the Girl Scout cookies to Julia and how Kurt loved to help people.

On the plane ride home from Houston, Sandy told Kurt that Julia was passionate about helping others. She informed him that Julia's organization donated money to purchase wigs for cancer patients.

"Wow, now that's something I'd like to do," Kurt said.

"I didn't know how you felt about it, you know, with you wanting to do something in memory of your dad," Sandy replied.

"We need to tell our team about this and get involved somehow," he said.

Kurt didn't do just that. Sandy retrieved more details about it from Julia and at their first monthly meeting, after they returned from Houston, Kurt had Sandy share about it. When it came time to explain why it was important to them, Sandy stopped and invited Kurt to take over.

Kurt paused for a moment. He was emotional and tried to regain his composure. He started to cry. No one had ever seen Kurt in any other emotional state except happy-go-lucky.

"A few years ago, my father died of cancer, and I determined right then, at his funeral, that I would do something to help other cancer patients in memory of my dad who . . ." Kurt started to weep, "Who was a mentor in his own right."

Kurt looked upward and said, "This is for you Dad. . ."

Everyone started crying, even the men! It was one of the most moving meetings in the history of Kurt's organization. Randy was there and he took the microphone and exhorted the group on behalf of Kurt and Sandy. He explained, "This is why we do what we do."

Randy took over the meeting. He was the guest speaker that night, and he announced that he had some good news to share. Kurt and Sandy were a few weeks away from their one-year anniversary with the company. Randy informed the group that a national conference was being held in Phoenix and that Kurt and Sandy would be on the stage as Diamonds!

The group gave them a standing ovation.

Kurt and Sandy had reached their goal . . . that month, they capped at $5,900 in monthly income. Kurt and Sandy were already aware of their achievement, but they rarely shared their totals. They allowed Randy to do the bragging. And he had no problem doing so.

~

The evening finally arrived. Sandy and Kurt purchased new outfits for the occasion. They were especially excited because they flew Bryan and Lorrie to Phoenix as well. They wanted them to celebrate too because they sacrificed to allow their parents to build the business over the past twelve months. Lorrie was dressed in an elegant gown and, amazingly, they talked Bryan into wearing a suit and tie.

When Bryan came out of his room to go to the meeting, he was wearing sneakers.

"Young man, you need to march right back into your room and change your shoes," Sandy demanded as all four stood in the hallway at the hotel.

"I can't . . . I forgot to pack them," Bryan said.

Sandy's mouth dropped wide open. She looked like she was ready to faint when. . .

"Bazinga!"

"What did you say?" Sandy exclaimed.

"Bazinga!" Bryan repeated.

Before Sandy had a heart attack, no pun intended, Lorrie interrupted and said, "Bazinga . . . It's what Sheldon says when he pulls a prank. It means *gotcha!*"

"Who's Sheldon?" Sandy demanded to know.

"Big Bang Theory," Bryan said.

Sandy stood silently mad.

"It's a TV show, Mom," Lorrie said.

Bryan pulled out his room key, inserted it into the slot of the door, and then turned around and said, "Bazinga!"

Kurt, Lorrie and Bryan busted out laughing. Sandy started to smile, but she had never seen the show, so she didn't really get the joke.

Bryan worked his way into the room. He could be heard through the wall laughing.

"It really is funny," Kurt said to Sandy. She still wasn't laughing.

"The show . . . the TV show . . . it's funny," Kurt said as to clarify that they weren't laughing at Sandy.

Bryan came out with his good shoes on. They got on the elevator and started to descend.

"Honey, did you tell them the cruise vacation is cancelled?" Sandy said to Kurt.

"What?" Bryan shouted.

"Bazinga!" Sandy exclaimed with emphasis on the "z."

They all busted out laughing, and it continued in the lobby.

~

Denny was at the podium. Randy and Melissa were standing next to Kurt and Sandy. They presented the Mercedes keys to them and pronounced them as Diamonds. They were one of several couples and individuals who received a Mercedes that night. But they were the only persons awarded that night who had accomplished that goal in one year. It was a Mercedes milestone.

Denny asked Kurt and Sandy to remain on the stage for a few more moments. They were awarded a plaque as Outstanding Sponsor of the Year. Then Denny presented them with a special reward.

"We are proud of this couple . . . and I can vouch for their success and tell you they are special people and dear to my heart. And, in honor of achieving the Outstanding Sponsor of the Year award, we present to you an all-expense paid trip for you and your family to the Caribbean Islands.

Immediately, Bryan and Lorrie jumped to their feet and started shouting, jumping, and high-fiving each other.

"In case you are wondering, those are their children," Denny explained.

The crowd broke out with laughter and cheered. Denny and Randy congratulated them for their achievement as the crowd gave them a standing ovation.

Julia topped off the night with a moving speech and a dinner afterglow that followed.

TWENTY-ONE

Life's a Beach

The decision was made. Kurt and Sandy waited three more months after being recognized as Diamonds. They wanted to be sure when to make the next step, so they consulted with Denny, and he recommended that they wait two to three months with a steady stream of income of at least $5,000 a month before resigning from the police force.

The statistics were calculated and they had averaged a little over $6,000 a month for the past three, so they sat down as a family and discussed it. They revisited the dream, set new goals, calculated a plan of action and mapped a course for the next twelve months on the calendar. They reviewed their financial situation, determined what things they would pay off, what expenses they would accrue, how to save and where to invest. Sandy and Kurt were not frugal, but neither were they frivolous with their decisions or money. They were used to a tight budget and making sacrifices.

Bryan and Lorrie thought the reward their parents received at Phoenix was the cruise they had discussed months earlier. However, the all-expense paid vacation presented to them for "Outstanding Sponsor of the Year" was in addition to the cruise Kurt and Sandy already booked in advance. After discussing it with Denny and Randy, their plans changed. Instead of taking the same or similar cruise vacation twice, Denny told Kurt and Sandy they would send them somewhere else.

After some discussion, Kurt and Sandy accepted their proposal and agreed to go to Panama City, Florida. Denny, Randy, Julia and another friend, Greg Hendricks, would often vacation together in Panama City, and it was highly recommended as a good vacation spot. So it was settled; they would take the Caribbean Island cruise first and then go to Panama City the following month.

Kurt and his family went on vacation to the Caribbean Islands. They embarked from Florida and sailed to the eastern Caribbean, including the Bahamas, St. Thomas, St. John, and St. Martin. They enjoyed the shops, fantastic beaches, horseback riding, snorkeling and jet skiing. This was the first of many vacations that Kurt, Sandy and the kids would enjoy in the years to come.

About a week after they returned from the Caribbean, Kurt submitted his resignation to his precinct. He gave a 30-day notice, but he only was required to fulfill two weeks out of four. On his last day, about 200 people from Kurt's team came to celebrate his crossover from employee to entrepreneur. Denny flew to Chicago and Randy organized the celebration party.

When Kurt exited the building, a limousine was waiting for him. He was escorted about three blocks from the precinct to a nearby park where they reserved a site for his grand day. He pulled up and saw all the people. He couldn't believe the number of friends that showed up. As soon as he climbed out of the limo, Randy and Denny were there, along with Sandy, Bryan, Lorrie, Mike Shell, and a host of close friends and associates. Denny handed Kurt a sledgehammer and Randy placed an alarm clock on the pavement.

Kurt knew exactly what to do. He had heard stories of this on the CDs, but this was his turn. Kurt slammed the hammer, demolishing the clock, signifying freedom from his job and never again would he have to set his alarm to go to work. Now he worked for himself. Everyone shouted, "FREEDOM," when Kurt smashed the clock.

Numerous pictures were taken of Kurt, Sandy, Denny and Randy that day. Almost instantly, the photos were posted on social media sites and the team's website as well. The smell of barbecue ribs and chicken filled the park with a tasty aroma. They even had blow-up playgrounds for the children. It was truly a great celebration. It took fifteen months to achieve, but Kurt and Sandy accomplished their first major dream, and some pictures on the refrigerator would be moved to the freezer side that night!

One month later, Kurt and Sandy and the kids were in beautiful Panama City. They were ready to spend seven days and nights at the luxurious InterContinental Playa Bonita Resort and Spa. The enormous hotel had over 300 rooms plus suites. It had two massive pools, large cabanas and views of the ocean and nearby mountains in the distance.

Historical land sites and ancient civilizations provided exploration tours for the visitors. The city offered an array of activities and attractions that Sandy and Lorrie intended on visiting while Kurt and Bryan went salt-water fishing and golfing at an 18-hole par 72 at the Tucan Club championship golf course.

On day two, Kurt and Sandy were resting under a cabana in the pool area. The night before, Bryan and Lorrie had met some kids their age, so they were enjoying themselves swimming in the pool.

Kurt's international phone rang. It was Denny.

"Hey, Kurt, I was just checking to see if the hotel I recommended is working out for you and Sandy," he said.

"Absolutely," Kurt replied. "Thank you so much Denny; I don't know what to say." Kurt activated the speakerphone feature.

"Don't mention it man, you deserve it."

Denny called him to discuss his manuscript. Kurt received grand praises and endorsements from Denny, which encouraged Kurt immensely. He truly was a mentor to the two of them, and his advice enabled him to leave his job two years earlier than expected.

"Here's a couple of things that I want to suggest to you and things to consider as you move forward with your rough draft," Denny said. "First, I would like to hook you up with a ghostwriter."

"A ghostwriter?" Kurt asked.

"Yes, I have a friend in Canada that has a publishing company. He's recommended someone to help you smooth out the rough edges of your content. Don't get me wrong, it's good. I just want to have a professional clean it up and make it flow better for the reader," Denny said.

"Whatever you say, Denny. I'm the novice here, so you point and I will follow," Kurt replied.

"I would like to write the foreword; Randy, Julia, and Greg will give endorsement, and I asked Steve Piston . . . he's the host of the Mastermind Event in Houston. . ." Denny said.

"The guy that looks like Dr. McCarty," Sandy interjected.

Kurt laughed silently when she said that and waved his hand to make her stop, lest he snickered noticeably.

". . . he hasn't given me an answer yet, that's because I haven't sent him a copy of the draft yet. But, I wanted to wait until we have the ghostwriter do his stuff first," Denny said.

"I'm honored," Kurt said.

"All right, I'll let you go and enjoy the sun . . . take care and see you when you get back in the States."

"Bye, Denny."

"Can you believe that?" Sandy said to Kurt.

Just then, a man who was sitting a few beach chairs down from them spoke up.

"Excuse me, I am sorry . . . I wasn't eavesdropping, but you had your phone on speaker, and I thought I heard the name Steve Piston."

"Yes, he was mentioned," Kurt said cautiously.

"Do you know him?" the man asked.

"I know of him, but I don't know him. He's a friend of my mentor."

"Well if you don't mind, who's your mentor?" the man asked.

Kurt wasn't sure where this was going; his suspicious tendency from being a homicide detective kicked in.

"Why do you ask?"

"I'm sorry . . ." The man got up, approached Kurt and Sandy, reached his hand in a friendly manner and said, "I'm Martin Syock. I'm a friend of Steve Piston. I spoke last year at the Mastermind Event in Houston. I thought maybe we'd crossed paths and hadn't had a chance to meet yet."

"Nice to meet you, Martin. This is my wife, Sandy, and I am Kurt Dungy."

"Nice to meet you, Sandy, and you, Kurt," he said with a smile.

"Sorry if I came off strong," Kurt explained. "I used to be a homicide detective, and I just retired from the force about a month and a half ago. I haven't adjusted yet."

"That's alright," Martin replied. "Do you mind if I sit down?"

"No, not at all, we're just enjoying the sun as our kids enjoy the pool with some friends."

"How many children do you have?"

"Two," Sandy piped in, "Bryan and Lorrie."

"Excellent," Martin said.

"And to answer your question . . . my mentor is Denny Harris."

"No kidding," Martin said with a chuckle in his voice. "I've known Denny for years. What an awesome guy."

"Yes, he is," Kurt responded affirmatively.

"So you're working on a book?" Martin inquired.

"Yeah, sort of. . ."

"Quite an undertaking . . . but well worth the effort," Martin said.

"He's been working on it for almost two years," Sandy replied.

"So, you two are in Denny's organization?"

"Yes, sir," Kurt answered.

"Please, call me Martin."

"Okay, Martin," Kurt replied.

"What level?" Martin asked.

"Just reached Diamond," Kurt answered.

"Congratulations," Martin responded.

"Thank you," Sandy added.

"Here on vacation?"

"Well, yes, but actually we won 'Outstanding Sponsor of the Year' in our company," Kurt replied.

"Wow, that's great."

"And you?" Sandy asked Martin.

"I've been here for 20 days. I leave tomorrow."

"Where's home?" Sandy inquired.

"Phoenix, I live in Phoenix . . . and to answer your question, I'm here working on my second book, called *Being Different*."

"What's it about?" Sandy asked.

"Well, as you know, many start on this journey, but not many stay the course. So, I wanted to write about dreams that overcome obstacles."

"That's sounds interesting," Sandy commented.

"Most network marketing strategies are based on 'how-to' formulas, but I want to write about being different. If we talk different, walk different, think different we will live different."

Martin, Kurt and Sandy sat under the shade of the cabana and talked for the next three hours. Bryan and Lorrie popped in to apply more sunscreen and to get some money to snack with their friends. It worked out great because their friends were leaving the next day, so the kids wanted to spend time at the pool together before their departure. This gave Kurt and Sandy time to get insights from Martin.

Kurt and Sandy picked his brain non-stop. Because Martin was from a different company, he had a few things that they had not heard of before and vice versa. Martin shared his story and how he made it in the industry. Many of the things he shared reminded Kurt of a book he read in his dream. But he chose not to ask or open that door.

When they finished talking, they exchanged phone numbers. Martin told Kurt that he would leave a copy of his first book at the front desk for him when he checked out.

The next morning, Kurt retrieved Martin's book, *Life's a Beach*. Kurt was taken aback because it was identical to the book he read in his vision called *Beach Money*. The book explained the system of residual income and ways to make money work for you . . . so you can sit on the beach and still be making money.

Later that night, out of the blue, Mike Shell called Kurt on his phone.

"Kurt, Mike Shell . . . so sorry to bother you on your vacation."

"That's okay, Mike." Kurt could tell in Mike's voice that something wasn't right. "What's going on?"

"Jim Coleman, he's in critical condition and it doesn't look good. If he can make it through the next 24 hours he has a chance."

"Oh my gosh!" Kurt gasped.

"What is it?" Sandy softly asked Kurt.

Mike continued, "He was in a major head-on collision."

Kurt covered the phone and whispered to Sandy, "It's Mike Shell . . . Jim Coleman's been in a car accident."

After Kurt and Sandy moved to their new home, Jim Coleman was Kurt's new partner and was with him the night Kurt was shot.

"What happened?" Kurt inquired.

"Jim was responding to a 10-55 and during the 10-80 an oncoming vehicle hit Jim."

Kurt thanked Mike for calling and they hung up. Kurt's mind raced back to the night he was shot. Even though he could not remember the events after he hit the ground . . . he remembered when he and Jim responded to the robbery.

Kurt told Sandy what Mike said . . . that Jim was responding to a call for an intoxicated driver and while in pursuit a vehicle drove through the intersection and hit Jim's cruiser head-on. Kurt and Sandy agreed that they should cut their vacation short and fly back to Chicago to be there with Jim.

The next day, Sandy contacted her friend, Michelle, who was a travel agent in Chicago, to see if she could book an earlier flight for them. The Tocumen International Airport is the only airport in Central America with two runways and it is a major hub for passenger traffic to Central America. Due to its busy traffic and tourism season, all the airlines were full, which would have forced Kurt, Sandy and their kids to go on standby with no guarantees, or they could wait two days for the next available flight. Two days was better than waiting for four, so they had Michelle rebook their return flight.

They continued to get updates from Mike. The two-day wait was difficult for Kurt, but it gave the kids some extra time at the resort pool and on the beach.

~

When Kurt and Sandy arrived at Midway, Mike was there to pick them up. Mike couldn't help but chuckle when he saw them. They were still in vacation attire — bright colors and thoroughly tanned. "Nice outfits," Mike said with a smirk.

"You're just jealous cuz you don't have a shirt like this," Kurt said with a smile.

It was about a 25-minute drive from the airport to the hospital. Jim had been in an induced coma since the accident, and they wanted to be there for Jim's wife, Linda. Then Mike took Bryan and Lorrie to a friend's house for the night in case Kurt and Sandy didn't come home until early in the morning. Mike was to return to the hospital after he dropped the kids off.

When they reached the CICU waiting room, several police officers, family and friends were with Jim's wife. Kurt and Sandy made their rounds, greeting one another.

When Mike returned from taking the kids, the only persons in the room were Kurt, Sandy and Linda. Mike had told Linda that Kurt and Sandy cut their vacation short in Panama City to come and see Jim. Linda thanked them for coming. She was overwhelmed by their compassion. Linda shared more details of Jim's situation and how the accident had happened.

They had small talk for about 30 minutes. Kurt told stories about Jim and their late night rides on patrol. Mike chimed in, sharing funny incidents that happened to him and Kurt while they were partners. The laughter seemed to take Linda's mind off of Jim.

It was approaching 10:00 PM and the cafeteria was about to close. So, Mike and Kurt decided to run down to the food court and get something to eat.

"Linda, would you like something from the cafeteria?" Mike asked.

She paused for a moment, "Sure, that would be great."

"Honey?" Kurt said looking at Sandy.

"A salad . . . if they have one," she answered.

"Me too," Linda said as she turned and smiled at Sandy.

The boys made their way to the elevator as Sandy and Linda remained in the CICU waiting room. It had been three days since the accident. Early that day, the swelling on Jim's brain receded drastically, so the doctors gradually withdrew the anesthetics, and they were waiting for Jim to regain consciousness. It had been about five hours, and no word had come from the nurses' station.

"I'm so sorry you had to cut your vacation short," Linda said.

"No need . . . we wanted to come sooner but we couldn't get an earlier flight," Sandy answered.

"Jim told me about Kurt leaving the precinct. Was it due to the shooting?"

"Yes . . . and . . . no," Sandy awkwardly replied.

"I'm sorry. I hope I didn't overstep my boundaries." Linda remarked as she lowered her head in embarrassment. "I should not have asked you that, I apologize."

"No . . . what I meant was, the shooting didn't force Kurt to quit, but it did provide the opportunity," Sandy said.

"Oh, my . . . was he let go?"

"No, he . . ." Sandy paused to think how she was going to answer Linda and appease her curiosity. "He kind of retired."

"Seriously! On a cop's pension?"

Sandy started to laugh and then oddly, Linda joined in too.

"Actually, after the shooting, Kurt and I restarted a home-based business and its growth financially allowed Kurt to quit the force."

"Wow!" Linda replied. "That's great . . . congratulations."

"Thank you," Sandy said.

"So how did the shooting fit into you and Kurt getting in this business?" Linda asked.

"Oh, it's a long story. Maybe I can get with you sometime soon and share it."

"I've got time now," Linda said enthusiastically.

"Linda, we're here for you and Jim. This isn't the time or place for me to be. . ."

Linda cut her off before she could finish. "No, please . . . it's helping me get my mind off Jim and besides, I really want to know what you did. Jim hates his job and the hours. . ."

"Yeah, the hours," Sandy agreed.

"Is your business something we could do too?"

Sandy sat still. *A hospital waiting room is not a place to share about the business*, she thought to herself.

"Please, Sandy. Tell me . . . I want to know how you did it."

~

Mike and Kurt got on the elevator. The doors closed.

"So, how was the trip?" Mike asked as the elevator declined to main floor.

"It was great."

"You deserved it, Kurt."

"You'll never guess who we met while we were in Panama City." Kurt proceeded to tell Mike about meeting Martin Syock and about the call from Denny concerning his book deal. Twenty minutes later, they returned to the waiting room with food in hand.

"Here you go . . . one salad and a water," Mike said as he handed it to Linda.

Before Kurt could hand Sandy her salad, Linda blurted out, "Kurt, tell me about your heart attack."

"What?!" Kurt said as he quickly turned his head toward Sandy.

THUD!

Kurt dropped Sandy's salad and it made a loud clamor when it hit the floor. Sandy and Linda busted out laughing as Kurt awkwardly bent down and attempted to put the spilled salad back into the plastic container.

"I'm so sorry," he said as he picked up the last tomato.

The girls continued to laugh. "I'll share mine with you," Linda said to Sandy.

"Did I miss something?" Kurt inquired as he tried to figure out where that question came from.

"I've been sharing our testimony with Linda, telling her about your MLM heart attack experience and how your shooting opened the door to our business." Sandy replied.

Kurt picked up the food container, placed it on the small table next to Sandy, and then inadvertently leaned into her ear to whisper. "Really, Sandy . . . Here? Now?"

Linda heard him. "It's okay, Kurt, I insisted she tell me."

"Okaaaay. . ." Kurt clumsily replied.

"Your story is amazing! You *need* to write a book," Linda said.

Simultaneously, Mike, Sandy and Kurt looked at each other. *Awkward*, Kurt thought to himself.

"Tell me more! Please sit down," Linda insisted as she pointed to a chair next to Sandy. "I want to learn more about your business and how it allowed you to quit your job."

Not knowing what to say, Kurt turned and looked at Sandy.

"I don't know where to start," Kurt responded.

"Well. . . You just woke up from Vegas," Linda replied.

Again, Kurt looked at Sandy. "I gave her the short version," Sandy remarked and then smiled back at Kurt.

"Tell me, what is 'CPR' and how did that help you with your business venture?" Linda inquired.

On the trip back to Chicago, Kurt couldn't sleep. So, he read a book on the plane. It was called *CPR for Network Marketing* by Julia McDaniel. What he read helped him understand the "why" and the "what" of his life, so he decided to share it with Linda.

"In the medical field, CPR stands for cardiopulmonary resuscitation. It's an emergency procedure which is performed in an effort to manually preserve intact brain function until further measures are taken to restore blood circulation and breathing when a person is suffering from cardiac arrest."

Kurt spent some time researching medical documents while writing his book, so this was fresh in his mind. It suddenly made sense and he was ready to articulate the meaning of his vision.

"It's a method used to bring someone back from the dead," Kurt explained. "In my business or the Multi-level Marketing industry, some people who attempt to succeed suffer setbacks, like a heart attack. They do the wrong things and don't do what's important to survive in this industry and they die, sort of speaking.

"That was me. Like a heart attack victim, I didn't eat the right food, or exercise and my arteries clogged. And I had what I call an MLM heart attack. But this is where the CPR comes in. 'CPR' in network marketing stands for *Community* and *Culture* . . . *Products* and *Prospecting* . . . *Relationships* and *Repetition*.

"You see, Linda, network marketing isn't just about making money . . . it's what you do with the money you earn. For instance, MLM CPR begins in your community. It's making a change . . . doing something for others.

"Every year, Girl Scouts came to my house to sell their cookies. I never said 'no' . . . and they knew it. So, I was invaded by ten or more young girls from the same Brownie troop. I was so impressed with their ambition and entrepreneurial drive, I bought their cookies and then gave them away to less fortunate people on the streets where I patrolled.

"My MLM team does charity work in our community and we've donated money to rebuild parks and funds to build playgrounds. The 'C' stands for *community* and *culture*. Some of my friends in the MLM industry give thousands, and some millions, of dollars every year to orphanages and shelters in foreign countries.

"Not only that, my MLM team, here in Chicago, gives thousands of dollars to an organization that provides free wigs to women and men who have lost their hair due to chemotherapy.

"'P' stands for *products* . . . products that are tested and proven to aid or have greater value in areas of health and well-being. 'P' also stands for *prospecting* . . . prospecting is the method of awareness and recruitment to enlist others with a cause for helping people . . . people who are less fortunate and helping people who are selling their 'Girl Scout cookies' to establish a home business that could provide freedom and financial benefits. Not to get rich, but to spend time with our families and do things we could never do if we worked a job, 9-5, 40 hours a week, 50 weeks a year and 40 to 50 years of our life. And when we retire, then what?

"'R' stands for *relationships* . . . relationships that provide support, comfort when we are hurting . . . like right now . . . you sitting in this ICU waiting room. MLM changed my personality and taught me to be a giver in life and not a taker.

"'R' also stands for *repetition* . . . repetition is the system of exchange. What someone has done for me, I now share with someone else. It's like the movie *Pay It Forward*. Someone you never knew did a kind act to someone else, who did it to someone else, who in turn did it for me, and now I do it for others.

"Unfortunately, when I first entered this business, I didn't know then what I know now. Back then, I wasn't following the system and I was headed toward an MLM heart attack or a collapse. I was abrasive, impatient, insensitive, and expected more out of others than what I was willing to give back to them.

"Maybe you don't remember, but I came over to your house several years ago and talked to Jim about joining the MLM industry, and I showed a presentation to him."

"I remember, Kurt," Linda said in a soft voice.

"Well, Jim said 'yes,' but I didn't put any effort into training, teaching or mentoring him. For that, I am so sorry and the first thing I want to do is apologize to Jim for letting him down."

Tears started to flow down Linda's face as Kurt shared his heartfelt compassion.

"And as you know, two years ago I was shot while on duty."

"Yes, Jim has never got over that," Linda said emotionally. "He has felt so guilty that he let you down and wasn't there for you. He told me about that night. After he handcuffed the man and placed him in the patrol car, he said he was out of air, and it took him a minute to catch his breath. Then he started running in your direction and then he heard shots. . . Jim has had nightmares, and he avoided you because the guilt was overwhelming."

Kurt had no idea any of this was going on with Jim. He thought he was the one avoiding Jim, being hard and abrasive, and deserting him without any support to build a successful MLM business.

"I'm sorry that I didn't do more for Jim, but we're here now, and I want a second chance to help both of you. The significant income we receive every month is a result of what I've learned. Sandy and I want to show you how I came back to life when it looked like I was dead. And if you'll let us teach you and Jim, we can show you the methods for MLM CPR and revive your dreams."

"Absolutely," Linda said. "I'm sure Jim will feel the same."

"Your husband is a fighter and he'll get through this and when he does, we'll be right here to help you guys," Sandy said as she gripped Linda's hand in support.

"I don't know how to thank you," Linda said as she accepted a tissue from Sandy. She wiped the tears from her eyes, "I can't tell you how much this means to me… this story is going to change our lives. I really believe that. It's no coincidence that you're here."

Just then, a nurse came out and greeted Linda. "Jim woke up and he's asking for you," the nurse said with a smile. The nurse led Linda back to Jim's room. Mike, Kurt and Sandy waited for her return.

Forty-five minutes had gone by when the electric doors to the CICU opened and Linda came walking out with her head down. With great concern, Kurt, Sandy and Mike stood to greet her. Linda looked stunned, her face white as if she had seen a ghost. She just stood there . . . silent.

"Linda?" Kurt softly replied.

"Linda, are you okay?" Sandy asked as she put her arms around her with comfort, expecting some bad news about Jim's condition.

"How's Jim?" Mike asked.

"He seemed alright at first, but when the doctor came in, Jim went berserk!"

"What happened?" Sandy inquired.

"I don't know. He was a little groggy, yet coherent. He recognized me and we talked. He seemed fine. He even got excited when I told him you guys were out here. But when the doctor came in and told him his condition, Jim told him to get out!"

"What! Why?" Kurt asked.

"I don't know. He insisted on seeing his doctor. And then, he started shouting, 'Where's Dr. J? I want to talk to Dr. J!' It was pure pandemonium. They made me leave the room. I don't understand."

Kurt looked at Sandy. She silently communicated to Kurt by shaking her head, letting him know that she didn't mention Dr. J to Linda. It was obvious what was happening, but Linda was unaware.

Mike grinned in dismay, "Unbelievable . . . It's just like. . ."

"Jim's going to be just fine," Kurt quickly interjected. "You'll see." Kurt looked at Mike, placed his index finger over his lips, giving him a soundless "Shhh" sign, signifying, "Don't say a word."

Linda lifted her head toward Kurt. He swiftly removed his finger from his mouth, as she almost caught Kurt silencing Mike, and said, "You think so?"

Kurt joined Sandy and hugged Linda, "No, I *know* so!"

THE END

ABOUT THE AUTHORS

Jordan Adler went from living in a 400 square foot room in Tempe, Arizona earning $14,000 a year, to becoming a multi-millionaire in a few short months. But before that he was involved in 11 companies in 10 years and never signed up one person. Not one! He's a 13 year overnight success!

This would-be rock star joined Toastmasters in 1981 and quit as soon as he realized he would have to speak in front of groups. On the way to teach his first class, he was secretly wishing to have a serious car accident so he would have a good excuse not to show up.

Today his success speaks for itself. He leads a team of over 60,000 distributors with another 1,500 or so joining monthly. He believes that everyone should align themselves with opportunities that throw off residual income. He coined the phrase "beach money," and then wrote a bestselling book with that same title. 100% of the profits from his book are used to help entrepreneurs start businesses in developing countries through a micro-financing program called Kiva (www.kiva.org).

These days when Jordan isn't hanging out at his mountain home, he is supporting his team and training and coaching new distributors to create passive income. He believes that anyone can compress a 30-year career into just three to five years. His hobbies include flying helicopters, real estate investing, and international travel. He splits his time between Las Vegas, Nevada; Chicago, Illinois; and Jerome, Arizona.

Jordan's monthly residual income is 5 times bigger than his annual pay the last time he had a job. He has made nearly $15 million in network marketing to date. More importantly, he has helped hundreds of entrepreneurs free themselves from the rat race and live their dream lifestyle.

Orjan Saele says: Your dreams are promises made from your future; and if you develop your abilities to your full potential, you will fulfill those promises!

Don't allow anybody to steal your dream.

God Bless,
Orjan Saele

www.orjansaele.com

~

Donna Johnson, a former swimming coach and single mom, has built one of the largest network marketing organizations in the world. This Wisconsin girl with no college degree now has over 1,000 leaders who have reached an Independent VP Leadership Position which earns them a symbolic White Mercedes Benz. More important, the dynamic culture of her team that she's lad for over 25 years is admired and respected in not only the network marketing profession, but also in the business community.

A pioneer of network marketing for over 30 years, she is considered one of the top leaders in a profession dominated by men. Donna sits on the Editorial Board of the profession's magazine *Networking Times*,

and she is a frequent contributor.

As a pioneer "Revolutionist" with Art Jonak, Orrin Woodward, Randy Gage, Ken Dunn, Örjan Saele and Jordan Adler; Donna is passionate about uniting the profession to become "the world class business opportunity."

While enjoying a residual income that could put her in "full retirement," she continues to lead a vibrant business, influencing entrepreneurs not just in her organization and company, but across the industry. She's considered a leader in messaging integrity & sustainability in the network marketing profession: "Doing the Right Thing, in the Right Way, for the Right Reason."

While fully engaged and passionate about her business, she considers her number one accomplishment as being "mom" and "nanna" to her 5 children and 3 grandchildren. Together, her family leads several entrepreneurial ventures including a bed & breakfast in Negril, Jamaica http://www.bananasgarden.com/, a "permaculture" community in Bayfield, WI, http://www.TheDraw.com/, and "Spirit Wings Kid's" http://www.spiritwings.com/ A charity that supports orphans around the world.

Donna and her family travel to India and Africa each year to generate support for Streams of Mercy orphanages that she and her organization support. Donna and her partner, Thomas, also a network marketer, reside in Arizona, Sweden, Wisconsin, and Jamaica, but you'll often find her sailing in the British Virgin Islands and traveling the world. Her children laugh that they have to check her FACEBOOK PAGE to see where in the world their mom is!

Donna's philosophy is 3-Dimensional Success:

    1) making a difference

    2) creating balance in your life

    3) financial peace

~

Ken Dunn is one of the leadership training world's up and coming great speakers and trainers. An incredible hunger to learn and teach others has led Ken successfully through five different professional careers in the past 25 years.

Ken began a policing career at the age of 18. He was involved in the policing world's most exhilarating and challenging disciplines, including undercover drug and surveillance work, S.W.A.T. team work, aggravated child abuse, frauds, aggravated assaults, illegal weapons smuggling and homicides.

The birth of Ken's first child left him yearning for a career change. In the next ten years, Ken opened four different home businesses in four different industries (importing, property management, mortgage and direct sales) and made millions of dollars from home in each profession.

In direct sales, Ken has assisted in building communities in excess of 250,000 people in over forty countries. Ken has helped dozens of families create new lives for themselves and significant seven-figure incomes. As well, Ken has consulted with several direct sales company owners to successfully launch and scale their businesses around the world.

In 2008, Ken published his first book, *Being the Change*, which attracted significant attention and sold thousands of copies. Ken has also published a number of popular audio and video training sets, which are now commonly used as reference tools in the direct sales and mortgage industries. Ken is a living example that a sharp focus on leadership development and relationship building will yield success in any endeavor.

Today, Ken regularly speaks to groups in the direct sales, mortgage, insurance and banking industries. He uses humor and his own experiences to inspire audiences around the world. Ken lives in Toronto, Canada, with his wife, Julie, and children Matthew and Laura.

www.kendunnleadership.com

The four authors of *MLM Heart Attack* recorded their conversation while sitting on a beach in the British Virgin Islands. This candid conversation is available for free in MP3 format at:

www.nextcenturystore.com/mlm-heart-attack/

www.NextCenturyPublishing.com